WHALES AND DOLPHINS

Ann Arbor
Science
Library

WHALES AND DOLPHINS

Everhard J. Slijper.

Postscript by John E. Bardach

170 p. : ill.

ANN ARBOR :

THE UNIVERSITY OF MICHIGAN PRESS, c 1976.

775nu8

Preface

Numerous passages in the Bible and in the classics of antiquity indicate that whales and dolphins have played on man's imagination from time immemorial. In all likelihood men were intrigued with these animals who lived in the world of the fish but who clearly revealed their mammalian character by their behavior. Their milieu was inaccessible; and the dimensions of their largest representatives were gigantic. What is more, only recently has it become possible to maintain dolphins in captivity and experiment with them. For all these reasons our knowledge of cetacean life was still meager in the 1920s, being confined to a knowledge of their bodily structure for the most part.

Scientific investigations in the last thirty years have greatly enlarged our knowledge of cetacean life. So it now seems proper to summarize the results in a form that will be comprehensible not only to the specialist but also to the interested layman. I should like to introduce the reader to these remarkable and fascinating animals and help him to understand them. I should like to point out how meager our knowledge still is in many areas and what remains to be explored. In particular, I should like to point out the relevance of the work done by biologists if we are to solve the problem of whale conservation; if we are to prevent the existing stock of whales from being overstrained by today's whaling industry.

E. J. SLIJPER

Contents

1. *Mankind and the Whale*

When man appeared on earth whales were already there, and we may assume that the first coastal dwellers took a deep interest in these remarkable animals which represented such an abundant food source. The oldest testimony to this interest is provided by rock carvings found at various sites in Norway which date from the neolithic period (ca. 2200 B.C.). Whale bones from the settlements of Alaska's first inhabitants indicate that man had already been engaging in whaling some 1500 years before the birth of Christ. Whales and dolphins were also portrayed frequently by the ancient Greeks and Romans. Dolphins, in particular, play an important role in numerous sagas and legends. As is the case today in the Mediterranean region, dolphins were hunted in some areas and protected as holy creatures in others. The great whale was not hunted in the Mediterranean at that time.

It certainly should not surprise us that the Norwegians are the oldest whalers, aside from the original inhabitants of Alaska. The soil of Norway offers only a limited food supply to man whereas its long coastline, splintered by thousands of fjords, has directed people's thoughts to the sea from time immemorial. We do not know when the Norwegians began to engage in whaling, but in the year 890 Ottar of northern Norway informed King Alfred of England that whales had been caught in the vicinity of Tromsö. Most likely the whales in question were Biscayan right whales. In those days they were plentiful in the North Atlantic and could be captured very easily.

On their excursions to the South the Normans probably instructed the inhabitants of Normandy in the art of whaling. Indeed it is possible that the Basques learned this art in turn from the inhabitants of Normandy. In any case the Basques hunted the Biscayan right whale from the eleventh century, first in the Gulf of Biscay and then over the whole North Atlantic. In the year 1578 thirty Basque whaling ships were sighted off Newfoundland. It was a very profitable industry in those days. The oil was used for lighting, and the baleens were in great demand for the corset industry since steel and rubber were not yet known.

Toward the end of the sixteenth century, the Englishman Jonas Poole (1583) and the Hollanders Heemskerk, Barendsz, and De Rijp (1596) sought in vain to find a passage to the Far East in the Arctic Ocean. It was during these voyages that their attention was drawn to the large stock of whales in the Arctic region. Not only the Biscayan right whale lived here but also the Greenland right whale (Fig. 1). These two right whales are slow swimmers, and their layer of blubber is so thick that the carcasses float on the water surface; hence these whales can be captured with primitive hunting equipment. But since the Greenland right whale resides mainly amid drifting icebergs, a whaling expedition to the Far North called for careful preparations over a period of years. It was not until 1611 that Thomas Edge sailed to the Spitsbergen region as the first English whaler. The first Dutch ship followed in 1612.

Initially the captured whales were processed on land in the Spitsbergen archipelago. Later, when only a few whales could be seen in the island bays, whalers scoured the entire Arctic Ocean and flensed the carcasses as they floated alongside the ship. The blubber was shipped in barrels to the countries of western Europe engaged in whaling. A productive industry developed there in many countries in addition to Holland and England. Expeditions from Norway, Denmark, and Germany (Hamburg, Bremen, Lübeck) participated in the "Greenland run." And in the eighteenth century Americans also joined in the hunt for the two right whales on both sides of their continent. In the year 1697, 1888 whales were caught by 182 ships of different nationalities in Spitsbergen alone. At the end of the nineteenth century baleen was still being sold for eight dollars per kilogram in San Francisco. The entire proceeds from a single Greenland right whale came to about eight thousand dollars.

Due to political and economic conditions in western Europe, whaling in northern waters dropped markedly at the end of the eighteenth century. Only the English, using constantly improved techniques, carried on this activity throughout the nineteenth century. By that time the stock in the North was so decimated that it was no longer profitable to hunt for Greenland and Biscayan right whales. Today these animals are protected by international agreement, and only local inhabitants may capture them. In Siberia people still make sled runners out of whalebone. Once upon a time they also used it to make watch springs.

There is no doubt that people hunted whales in many other parts of the world from the sixteenth to the eighteenth centuries. We know, for example, that the Indians on the west coast of North America hunted Biscayan right whales, sperm whales, and gray whales. We also know that this industry has played an important role in the Japanese economy since 1616. Like the Norwegians, the Japanese population cannot live off the yield of agriculture and animal husbandry. They too need the sea as a source of food. The thousands of small islands off the coast make Japan an ideal location for whaling. Countless striking pictures in full color depict the ways and means by which whales were netted, most of them being Biscayan right whales, gray whales, and humpback whales (Fig. 1).

As the demand for whale oil and baleen grew steadily at the beginning of the eighteenth century, people tapped

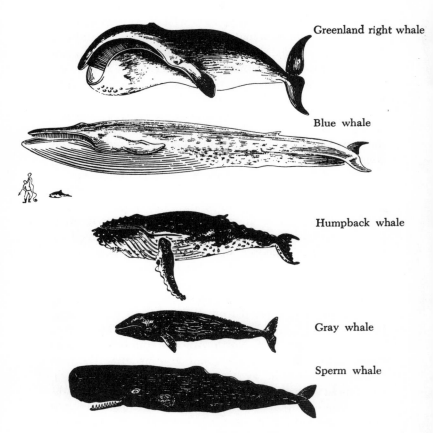

Greenland right whale

Blue whale

Humpback whale

Gray whale

Sperm whale

FIG. 1. Some of the large whales.

a new source of these products. The whalers of New Bedford and Nantucket extended their coastal industry. From
1721 to the middle of the nineteenth century they joined
the French, Portuguese, and English in exploring all the
seas and oceans of the world. Besides hunting southern
right whales and humpback whales, they also concentrated on sperm whales (Fig. 1) because the latter can
readily be captured with primitive hunting devices. The
romantic stories about Moby Dick, Timor Tim, New
Zealand Jack, and other whales who cost so many human
lives have to do with a relatively small number of old and
dangerous bulls. Most sperm whales can be killed with
almost little effort.

Since 1846, however, the catch of sperm whales plum-
meted. The growing cotton industry and gold fever in
America lured thousands of sailors from their ships. The
discovery of petroleum in Pennsylvania (1859) tolled
the death knell of sperm whaling because petroleum was
a better and cheaper light source than sperm oil. Yet it
was not until 1925 that the last whaling ships, the "John
M. Manta" and the "Margarett," returned to New Bedford from their last expedition. The sperm whale is
present in all the seas of the world, but it resides mainly
in tropical and subtropical waters. Hence expeditions
hunting sperm whales usually lasted many years; and
more than one sailor abandoned ship on some lush south
seas island to begin a new life with a dark-eyed native
maiden.

The latter half of the nineteenth century was the most
peaceful time that whales had known since the year 1600.
Only in a few places, e.g., Norway, Japan, and California,
were large whale catches recorded by shore stations. In
Norway and England, however, there had been repeated
attempts to hunt the very swift rorquals (*Balaenopteridae*), whose carcasses sink when they have been killed.

FIG. 2. Head of explosive harpoon and harpoon line on the bow of a Japanese whaler.

This group includes the blue whale (Fig. 1), the fin whale, and the sei whale[1] which, like the much slower humpback whale, are found in all the seas of the world. Only after steamships became available, and only after Svend Foyn of Tönsberg had invented the first practical harpoon gun with an explosive head in 1868 (Fig. 2) did

---

1. The sei whale is so named because it frequently appears with the sei fish (or coalfish) along the Norwegian coast.

it become possible to bring down the swift rorquals. The explosive charge is located in front of the prongs at the head of the harpoon. It explodes in the whale's body, and it can kill the whale in seconds when the shot is well placed. The cascass is then pumped up by an air tube so that it cannot sink.

Foyn's invention led to the rapid growth of shore stations, not only in Norway but also in Iceland, the Faeroe Islands, Japan, and other parts of the world. Nevertheless the demand for whale oil exceeded the supply at the end of the nineteenth century because important discoveries by Koch and Pasteur in the fight against disease carriers led to an extraordinary population increase in Europe and North America. Since the welfare of these peoples also improved greatly, there was a great demand for soap and margarine. In 1905 the process of fat hardening enabled people to convert unsaturated fatty acids into saturated ones. This allowed whale oil to be used in making margarine. Consequently, the whale industry had to look for new supply sources.

Cook, Ross, Weddell, and other explorers told repeated tales of enormous whale stocks in the waters of Antarctica. In 1904, therefore, C. A. Larsen established Grytviken shore station on South Georgia. By 1910 there were six shore stations on South Georgia and on the South Shetland, South Orkney, and South Sandwich Islands. Fourteen factory ships (most of them Norwegian) with forty-eight catcher boats lay at anchor in the island coves. Licenses in this English territory were very costly, however, and the whale stock in the immediate vicinity of the islands decreased. In 1923 whalers began to use factory ships that could do their work on the open sea (Figs. 3 and 4). The first "floating cookery" which could take the whale carcass on board through a stern slipway was built in 1925, and the heyday of Antarctic whaling came in the 1930s when 41 factory ships with their catcher

FIG. 3. Flensing a fin whale on the quarter deck of the Dutch factory ship *Willem Barendsz.* The layer of blubber has just been removed. Photo by W. L. van Utrecht (Amsterdam).

boats were operative in Antarctic waters. Most of these ships were Norwegian.

Many ships were lost in World War II. During this time people also recognized that the whale stocks had been strained too severely. For these reasons the number of expeditions was reduced to about twenty by the end of the war. It now seems that the center of gravity has shifted from western Europe to Japan insofar as Antarctic whaling is concerned. In the 1960–61 season the Antarctic fleet consisted of 9 Norwegian, 2 English, 3 Russian, 1 Dutch, and 7 Japanese expeditions.

The chief product of present-day whaling is still whale oil. It is used mainly for human nourishment but it is also used in the soap industry, in the leather and linoleum industry, and in the manufacture of synthetic resins. The

FIG. 4. Processing a rib piece on the foredeck of the *Willem Barendsz*. Photo by W. L. van Utrecht (Amsterdam).

oil of the sperm whale cannot be used in the manufacture of margarine and soap because it is not a fat in the strict sense but rather a waxlike compound, i.e., the glycerol is replaced by monovalent alcohols of a higher molecular structure. Like the spermaceti from the powerful head cavity of the sperm whale, sperm oil is used for pharmaceutical and cosmetic purposes. It is one of the usual ingredients of skin creams, rouges, and lipsticks. Sperm oil is also used as lubricating oil, and in Japan it is used in the making of shoe polish (Fig. 5).

Sperm whale meat cannot be used as human food, but baleen whale is very tasty, being somewhat like beef. On most modern factory ships the lean portion of meat is deep frozen and carried off in refrigerator ships. The major portion of whale meat is eaten in Japan, where it is cooked in a savory manner. In western Europe some of it is eaten by human beings and some of it is used for dog food. Among the important suppliers of whale meat in western Europe are the shore stations in Norway, Iceland, and the Faeroe Islands. As dried meat meal, whale meat can also be used for fodder.

From the whale bones we make glue, gelatin, or bone meal which is used as artificial manure. Extremely good brushes can be made from the baleen, but these brushes are so impervious to wear and tear that the baleen industry is not interested in making them. In Japan whalebone is still used in the corset industry (Fig. 5). In western Europe it is now found only in certain riding boots and in the busbies of the British and Danish guards. Other byproducts of modern whaling are vitamin A from the liver oil, threads from the connective tissue, e.g., stitching thread or strings for tennis rackets, hormones from different organs with inner secretions, ivory from the teeth of the sperm whale, and ambergris which shows up now and then in the intestine of the sperm whale as the result of some pathological condition.

In the years following World War II approximately 35,000 whales have been captured annually in Antarctic waters. This figure includes about 25,000 fin whales and 8000 blue, sei, humpback, and sperm whales. Added to this is the yield of about fifty shore stations, so that a total of about 44,000 whales have been taken annually. The oil yield amounts to only about 2 percent of the fat

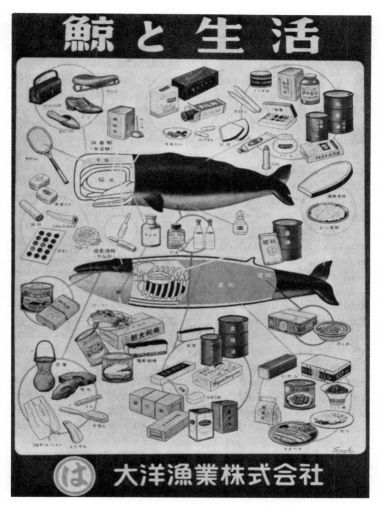

FIG. 5. Products made in Japan from sperm and fin whales.

production in the whole world, and to only about 5 percent of the world's production of animal fats.

Reading these figures we can readily see that conservation circles the world over are not the only ones concerned about the decrease in the stock of whales. Participating governments, too, have joined together to adopt measures designed to insure that the whale will continue to be a source of food for our descendants. In 1924 and 1927 the League of Nations tried to tackle this problem, but without success. The Geneva Convention was signed on 18 January 1936, and the London Convention was promulgated on 8 June 1937. After World War II nations engaged in whaling joined to form the International Whaling Commission in Washington on 2 December 1946. At present eighteen nations are represented on this commission: Argentina, Australia, Brazil, Canada, Denmark, England, France, Iceland, Japan, Mexico, the Netherlands, New Zealand, Norway, Panama, South Africa, Sweden, the Soviet Union, and the United States. On 11 August 1952, a special convention was formed by Chile, Ecuador, and Peru.

The International Whaling Commission has set forth numerous stipulations with regard to whaling. There is a limited season and certain areas are off limits. Right whales and gray whales may not be caught, and a minimum size for the other whales is in effect. Females with calves are protected, and so forth. But the most perplexing problem faced each year by the commission is to determine what should be the total whale catch allowed to expeditions operating in the waters of Antarctica. In recent years it has amounted to approximately 15,000 Blue Whale Units, this unit being 1 blue whale, or 2 fin whales, or 6 sei whales, or 2½ humpback whales. Unfortunately, it is not possible to protect pregnant females, or even females in general, because one can only determine the sex after the animal has been harpooned. Only in the

case of the sperm whale is there a noticeable difference
in length between the two sexes. Hence there is only one
important stipulation with regard to sperm whales: it is
forbidden to shoot sperm whales of less than 11.6 meters
(38 feet) in length. Proper compliance with the terms of
the international convention is checked by inspectors of
each nation on board the factory ships. In 1960, an international inspection setup was established.

The aforementioned stipulations obviously presuppose
precise knowledge of the whale's living and procreative
habits (see chapters 11 and 12). In past centuries countless researchers explored the anatomy of the porpoise and
other small Odontoceti. Among the first were Belon
(1553) and Bartholinus; in 1654 the latter dissected a
porpoise in the presence of King Frederick III of Denmark. Some information on the structure and living habits
of the great whales was provided by Zorgdrager (1728),
Fabricius (1780), John Hunter (1787), and William
Scoresby (1820). But on the whole we can say that the
hundreds of thousands of whales captured in previous
centuries contributed very little to a better knowledge of
their biology. The comparative anatomists of the nineteenth century—Camper, Vrolik, Van Beneden, Eschricht,
Turner, and Kükenthal, to name a few—made important
contributions to a better understanding of the structure
and physiology of the whale. But they contributed little
to our knowledge of reproductive biology and population
dynamics among whales.

It was only in the 1920s that practical research along
these lines was started in England and Norway. Since
then special research institutes have appeared in England,
Norway, Holland, Australia, Canada, the Soviet Union,
and Japan. They have assembled much important data
connected with solving the problems involved in preserv-
ing our whale stock. A very important institute is the
Bureau for International Whaling Statistics in Sandefjord,

Norway. Each year it publishes detailed statistical data on the world's whale catch. The results of this practical research and its importance for international conservation measures will be discussed in more detail in chapter 12.

ii. External Appearance and Whale Origins

Today any school child can tell us that whales and dolphins are not fishes but mammals. Four hundred years before Christ, Aristotle informed people that the cetaceans possess hair and breathe with lungs rather than with gills; that the young develop inside the mother's body and are nourished with her milk after birth; and that these animals have a horizontal tail fin rather than a vertical one like fishes and reptiles. Nevertheless Aristotle placed the cetaceans with the fishes in his systematic classification, as did Pliny (around the time of Christ's birth), Belon (1553), and Rondelet (1554). This is due to the fact that these authors used the milieu in which animals lived as the basis of their zoological classification. John Ray was the first to classify the cetaceans as mammals in 1693. Linnaeus went further and divided them into toothed whales (*Odontoceti*) and baleen whales (*Mystacoceti*); the latter possess no teeth and capture their food with the help of their baleen or whalebone.

Among the baleen whales further subdivisions are made. There are the right whales with a dorsal fin and long baleen, without grooves on the ventral side and without a dorsal fin (Greenland right, Biscayan right, pigmy right). There are the gray whales (*Eschrichtiidae*), with a short baleen and two to four grooves and without a dorsal fin (the California gray whale of the North

15

Pacific). And there are the rorquals (*Balaenopteridae*) with short baleen, a dorsal fin, and seventy to one hundred grooves on their ventral side (blue whale, fin whale, sei whale, Bryde's whale, humpback whale, and lesser rorqual; see Figs. 1 and 14).

The toothed whales include both sperm whales (*Physeteridae*) and bottlenose whales (*Ziphiidae*), which feed mainly on cuttlefish, as well as dolphins in the stricter sense (*Delphinidae*), river dolphins (*Platanistidae*), and porpoises (*Phocaenidae*, Fig. 6) whose main food is fish even though certain species eat a great deal of cuttlefish.

The general body form of the whale is that of a fish or a torpedo. It is a streamlined form which ensures the least possible resistance to the water (Figs. 6 and 14). The hide is smooth; only on the jaw are there hairs or the rudiments of hair, and these are in the nature of sensory cilia. To ensure water runoff along the whole body, practically all the bodily organs which protrude on the bodies of other mammals are built into this streamlined form. There are no external ears and no protruding nipples; indeed the external parts of the posterior limbs are absent entirely. In 20 mm. long embryos one can still find clear outlines of posterior fins (Fig. 7), but these have disappeared by the time the embryo reaches a length of 30 mm. The posterior limbs are represented solely by a very simple, rod-shaped pelvic bone which has no direct connection with the vertebral column (Fig. 6). Right whales still bear traces of a thigh bone (femur). These rudiments, and even fin rudiments protruding from the body, are also found in other whales; but it is a rare and abnormal case. By contrast the anterior limbs are always full grown, developing into flat flippers of greater or lesser length. These limbs still possess all the skeletal elements of a normal foreleg and, like the hind legs, they show up in young embryos as normal mammalian limbs.

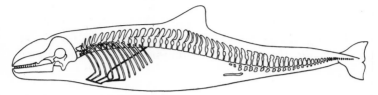

FIG. 6. Schematic diagram of the skeleton of a common porpoise (without the flippers). Note the rudiment of a pelvis and the position of the diaphragm.

This fact indicates that the cetaceans are descendants of normal land-living mammals. Studies of the chemical composition of their blood albumen have shown that they are probably most closely related to the carnivores and ungulates among the mammals. In particular, they seem to be closely related to the artiodactyls (cows, camels). In all probability the cetaceans, along with the carnivores and ungulates, sprang from a group of small insect-eating carnivores (*Insectivora-Creodonta*), which lived in the Cretaceous period some 125 million years ago.

FIG. 7. An 8 millimeter long embryo of the common porpoise. Note the rudiments of anterior and posterior limbs. After Müller (1920).

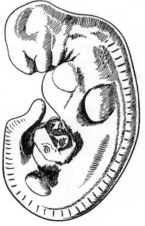

FIG. 8. Schematic reconstruction of an ancient whale ancestor (*Basilosaurus*), which lived in the sea 35 million years ago in what is now the state of Alabama.

We do not possess a single fossil of the transitional forms between the aforementioned land animals and the whales. The oldest representatives of the cetaceans, whose remains from the Eocene epoch (about 45 million years ago) have been found in North America, Egypt, New Zealand, and Nigeria, are already aquatic animals. These ancient whale ancestors (*Archaeoceti,* Fig. 8) were two to twenty meters long, possessing a partly serpentine and a partly dolphinlike shape. But they also evince a number of primitive features which point to their derivation from land mammals. The anterior limbs, for example, are much less markedly finlike in character whereas the pelvis has a clearcut articular cavity for the articular head of the femur—the latter also being present. A typically primitive feature is also the position of the nasal opening.

The nasal opening of the whale is called the blowhole. In very young embryos (4 to 5 mm. long) it is located on the tip of the snout as in all land mammals. By the time the embryo has attained a length of 22 mm., however, the blowhole has shifted so far back that it is at the same spot where it is located on adult whales, i.e., on top of the head behind the real snout itself (Fig. 9). Why the nasal opening lies at this spot is not fully clear, but we have the impression that it is connected with the distribution of weight in the whale's body. As figure 10 shows, the position of a mammal floating in water is determined by two opposed forces: the downward force of gravity and the upward force of buoyancy. In relationship to the position of the lungs, the pivot of buoyancy is always farther toward the head than that of gravity. This gives rise to a torque, and the animal rotates until both points are vertically under one another. The result is an oblique position in the water, with the tip of the

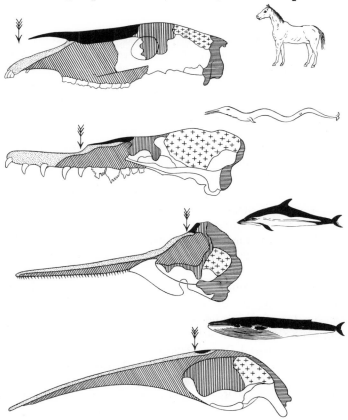

FIG. 9. Skull of a horse, an ancient whale ancestor, a toothed whale (dolphin), and a baleen whale (fin whale), to show the backward shift of the nasal opening and the telescoping of the skull bones. Dotted: intermaxillary bone; black: nose bone; vertical hatchline: frontal bone; diagonal hatchline: superior maxilla; cross pattern: parietal bone; horizontal hatchline: occipital bone.

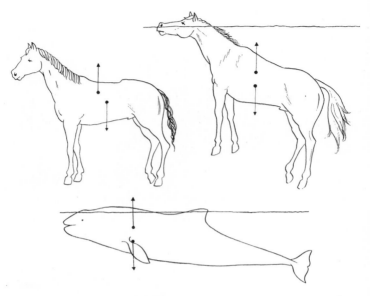

FIG. 10. Position of a horse and a porpoise in water, caused by the torque resulting from the forces of gravity and buoyancy.

snout just above the water line. With the exception of human beings and anthropoid apes, therefore, a mammal does not drown when it falls into water, or at least it does not drown right away.

With whales the case is different. When the center of gravity and the pivot of buoyancy lie vertically, the whale's body has an almost horizontal position. This can often be seen quite well when a whale or dolphin is slumbering or slowly surfacing (Fig. 11). In this position the tip of the snout is under water, and only the middle and back portion of the head jut out. Hence the latter areas provide the most suitable spot for the outlet of the nasal duct, i.e., the blowhole. Only in the sperm whale does the nasal opening lie far forward atop the cushion of sperma-

FIG. 11. Sperm whales surfacing off the coast of New Guinea. Note their almost horizontal position. Photo by R. Stephan.

ceti. Here we seem to be dealing with a more recently developed feature that is connected with the development of the spermaceti cushion because the nasal ducts, which are surrounded by bones, are located in exactly the same part of the skull as they are in other whales.

With the shift of the nasal opening backward and upward, and with the elongation of the jaw which is connected with the development of teeth rows in the *Odontoceti* and baleen rows in the *Mystacoceti,* certain alterations in the mutual positioning of the skull bones also occurred. The bone of the nose shifted toward the back while the superior maxilla and intermaxillary bone grew farther back. Thus they were pushed over and, in the case of baleen whales, partly under the frontal bone, while the parietal bone was crowded completely to one side (Fig. 9).

This telescoping of the skull bones had not yet taken place in the first whale ancestors, but their nasal opening no longer lay on the tip of the snout. It lay half way be-

tween the spot it occupies on recent whales and the spot
it occupies on land mammals. Telescoping shows up in
only one of the more recent ancestors of the whale, *Patrio-
cetus,* an animal several meters in length from the upper
Oligocene sands of Linz. This telescoping appears to be
exactly the same as that found in the baleen whales. In
other characteristics as well (e.g., the course of the arterial channels in the region of the posterior lumbar
vertebra and the anterior caudal vertebra) there is extensive agreement between the first whale ancestors and
the baleen whales. To be sure, there are arguments
against the direct descent of baleen whales from the
first primitive whales; but it is well established that the
first whale ancestors are much more closely related to the
baleen whales than to the toothed whales.

The presence of a well-developed set of teeth in the
proto-whales certainly need not contradict this thesis because the baleen whales definitely had forefathers with a
well-developed set of teeth. Take the case of baleen
whale fetuses, specifically those of the fin whale. When
the fetus ranges from thirty to three hundred centimeters
in length, that is, when it is three to eight months old, we
find a set of tooth buds (Fig. 12) which are completely
reabsorbed in older fetuses when the rudiments of the
baleen appear. Many of these tooth rudiments have the

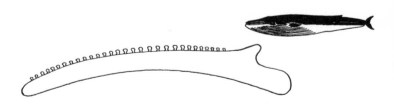

FIG. 12. Right lower jaw of a fin whale fetus (128 centimeters
long) with tooth buds.

tricuspidate crowns that are characteristic of the teeth of the proto-whales. Moreover, in their overall structure and in their construction the dentures of the proto-whales are strongly reminiscent of the dentures of a recent seal from the waters of Antarctica which feeds almost exclusively on crustaceans (*Lobodon carcinophagus*). If we assume that many whale ancestors fed on crustaceans, then this common food would be another piece of evidence pointing to a closer relationship between the first whale ancestors and baleen whales.

The oldest fossil baleen whales are known from a period when the first whale ancestors had not yet become extinct, i.e., the middle Oligocene (ca. 30 million years ago). They are authentic though primitive baleen whales without any trace of teeth in the adults. The most surprising feature of fossils from the Oligocene and Miocene is their modest length, ranging from only 2.75 to 9.75 meters. In the Pliocene (ca. 7—1 million years ago) the right whales had already attained their present-day length (5 to 15 meters). But the rorquals from the Pliocene deposits of Antwerp and the eastern Netherlands had a length of from 3.5 to 15 meters; they were certainly much smaller than their present descendants which range from 9 to 33 meters in length.

The oldest known remains of toothed whales come from the upper Oligocene (27 million years ago). In general their measurements gradually increase too, and a marked asymmetry develops in the skull. The skulls of the oldest Odontoceti are still completely symmetrical. Among species from recent geologic time, however, certain bones on the right side have developed far more than those on the left side. Their blowhole can assume a surprisingly asymmetrical position (Fig. 13). How this asymmetry arose is still unexplained. In the rest of their build these animals have exactly the same symmetrical proportions as land mammals do. In fact their heart and lungs are constructed more symmetrically than those of land mammals.

Now that we have briefly treated the origins and kinship of the cetaceans, we shall conclude this chapter with a few remarks on several features of their external appearance. We will start with their color. The beluga whale has a yellowish white color, while the narwhal is yellowish brown with dark spots. Most other whales and dolphins are completely black (right whale, sperm whale, pilot whale); or else—and this is the most common pattern by far—they have a black top side and a white underside. This pattern of color distribution is commonly seen in fishes and many land animals too. When light shines on them from above, the animal gives the impression of

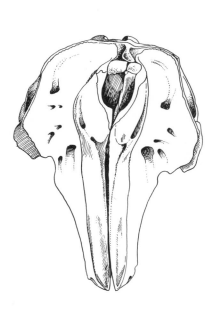

FIG. 13. Skull of a female narwhal to show the asymmetrical bone development. After van Beneden and Gervais (1880).

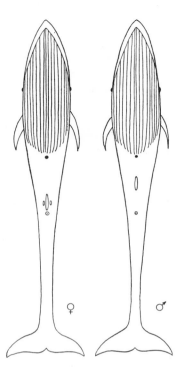

FIG. 14. Schematic drawing of a female and male fin whale from the ventral side.

being pretty uniformly colored and blends into its surroundings because the dark top side reflects little light while the underside in shadow reflects a great deal. This phenomenon is called "countershading."

Color differences between the sexes have not been found in whales, and other external differences are also insignificant. Adult female baleen whales are one to two meters longer than males on the average. Just the opposite is usually true for toothed whales, although the difference in length can range from a few centimeters to six meters (sperm whale). In the case of the bottlenose whale and the killer whale there are also clearcut differences in the development of the forehead cushion and the dorsal fin. The difference between the sexes can be seen only when we get a look at their ventral side. Figure 14 indicates that the slit in which the penis lies is about halfway between the anus and the navel whereas the female genital opening is directly ahead of the anal opening.

The grooves of the rorquals, also indicated in figure 14, extend just about to the navel in both sexes and most species. Their significance is not yet completely clear. As yet we have not been able to establish any connection of them with hydrodynamics. Therefore, it seems most likely that they are somehow related to the enlargement of the mouth during food intake (see chapter 8).

III. *Swimming*

Whales and dolphins live mainly in the secret recesses of the deep. Yet the sea voyager sights them more often than fish because they are compelled to surface for breathing. An escort of dolphins at the bow of a ship (Fig. 15) is a familiar sight to the seaman, and even the large whales may be sighted now and then. On rare occasions the encounter may take on a dramatic character, i.e., when the ship's bow collides with a whale sleeping near the surface. In such cases the whale is usually so critically wounded that it is doomed to die; while the ship must get free of the carcass before it can continue on its journey. In all the collisions that have been known to take place, the whale in question has been a sperm whale; it apparently can sleep pretty soundly. One often encounters right whales and humpback whales sleeping or snoozing on the surface of the water. The other rorquals seem to be more active, but now and then they too may be seen sleeping in tropical waters.

Usually these animals are seen only when they come to the surface to breathe, and then they are only visible for a few seconds. When the great whales are swimming slowly, they come to the surface in an almost horizontal position; when they are swimming fast, their position is much more oblique and they make a somersaultlike turn. At that time one can see a large portion of their back and tail above the surface of the water (Figs. 16, 17). It is only in this brief instant that a whale can be shot by the

FIG. 15. Two Arabian dolphins (*Tursiops aduncus*) before the bow of a ship off Djibouti. Note the open blowholes and the torpedo shape of their bodies. Photo by Captain W. F. J. Mörzer Bruins.

FIG. 16. A fin whale surfacing in a semicircular pattern. Note the flukes near the center of the picture. Photo by W. L. van Utrecht (Amsterdam).

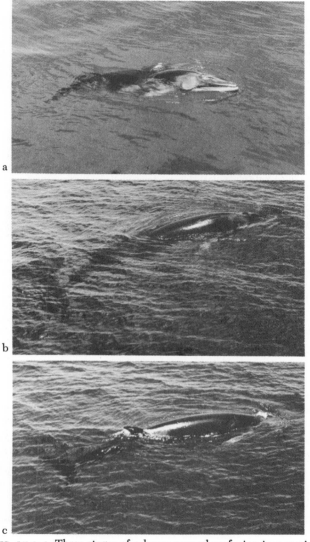

FIG. 17 a–c. Three stages of a lesser rorqual surfacing in a semi-circular pattern in the harbor of Réunion. Photos by Captain W. Peeters.

FIG. 18. A humpback whale leaping out of the water.
After Glassell (1953).

whale hunter. Right whales, gray whales, humpback
whales, and sperm whales usually show their flukes above
the water when they dive, and always when they go into
a deep dive (Fig. 25). The flukes of the other baleen
whales usually remain under water.

All cetaceans are playful animals, often springing up
out of the water as they move along. Dolphins ordinarily
leap over the water in a relatively shallow arc; but they
can also shoot vertically up into the air with their whole
body. Among the great whales there is one in particular
that is a real acrobat; the humpback whale will frequently
leap completely out of the water and even execute somer-
saults (Figs. 18, 19). It also likes to beat the water with
its pectoral flippers, reminding the onlooker of the sails
of a windmill. Sperm whales, too, will frequently leap
partially or completely out of the water. One sees this
less frequently in the case of the large rorquals, but it
has been observed on occasion.

In normal swimming the flippers of cetaceans play only a minor role, if any at all. Their forward movement in the water depends completely on the movements of the tail with its flukes, i.e., on the portion of the body behind the anal opening. In the large aquariums of the United States films have been made of porpoises, dolphins, and a pigmy sperm whale swimming under water. These films have shown that the tail moves up and down quite vertically

FIG. 19. Sketch of the somersault of a humpback whale, based on what was observed by two merchant marine officers, Bannan and Hermans, off the east coast of Australia.

FIG. 20. Pacific white-sided dolphins swimming in the Marineland Aquarium (California). The different position of their tails indicates the vertical movement of this organ. The oblique position of the flukes is clearly noticeable on the back dolphin.

(Fig. 20). Studies of constraints to movement in the dolphin's body have confirmed the film results; and they have shown that the vertical motion of the tail takes place mainly in the region of the base of the tail near the anus. A second center of motion lies in the area where the tail turns into flukes (Fig. 21).

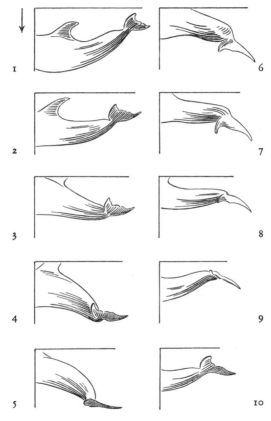

FIG. 21. Ten frames of a film taken of a bottlenose dolphin swimming in the Florida Marineland Aquarium. 1–5: downbeat stroke of tail. 6–10: upbeat stroke of tail. Altered illustrations by Parry (1949).

Closer analysis of the film shots has shown that in both the upbeat and the downbeat the fluke section lags a bit, so that it slightly angles vis-à-vis the rest of the tail. Thus the force produced by the resistance of the water is directed diagonally upward and forward on the downbeat and downward and forward on the upbeat (Fig. 22). Because the upward and downward components cancel each other out, the overall outcome of one full beat is a force that drives the whale forward. Forward movement depends almost completely on the forces produced by the movement of the fluke section. The rest of the tail, highly oval in shape because it is compressed on the sides, cuts the water like a knife and hence offers minimal resistance. If the reader has trouble seeing that such a small surface as that of the fluke can propel the whale's whole body, then he should take a look at the propeller of some huge ocean liner in drydock sometime and note how really small it is.

What speeds do whales and dolphins attain in their swimming? To answer this question we must first realize

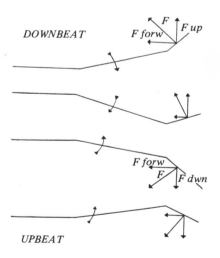

DOWNBEAT

UPBEAT

FIG. 22. Schematic drawing of the forces at work in the up and down movement of a dolphin's tail. The force (F), which arises from the resistance of the water, can be divided into several components: a forward component (F forw), and an alternatingly upward (F up) and downward (F dwn) directed component.

that two kinds of performances are to be distinguished here. Maximum speed over a short run period, akin to a sprint, must be distinguished from the normal speed that a whale or dolphin can maintain for hours.

Right whales, gray whales, and humpback whales are certainly slow swimmers. Their maximum speed is about 6 knots (10 knots in the case of the humpback whale), and their normal speed is 2 to 3 knots.[1] Sperm whales are much faster, their normal speed being about 10 knots and their maximum speed about 20 knots. But even they fall short of the performance of the rorquals, with their normal speed of 12 to 14 knots. The top speed of fin and sei whales has been recorded at 35 knots. Without a doubt the differences between different species is related to their overall bodily form and to the thickness of their layer of blubber. In right whales the latter comes to about 50 centimeters, in sperm whales to about 16 centimeters, and in rorquals to about 10 centimeters. If the right whales were to move at the same speed as the rorquals, they would certainly die of heat exhaustion.

Freshwater dolphins on the average have a maximum speed of 10 knots and a normal speed of 2 to 3 knots. But porpoises and dolphins can show a normal speed of about 20 knots, and on sprints they could certainly attain higher speeds. These animals and the rorquals can thus keep up with our modern passenger steamships, and they far outstrip the speed of a nonatomic submarine (8 knots under water).

The most striking and noteworthy feature of all this is that the speed of the smaller porpoises and dolphins is exactly the same as that of their relatives who may outstrip them a thousandfold in volume or weight. Insofar as ships are concerned, we all know that speed generally increases with the tonnage. This puzzling fact, known as

---

1. A sea mile (a knot) is 1851.85 meters.

Gray's paradox, was closely studied during recent decades by English researchers at the Cambridge zoological laboratory and elsewhere. The paradox is explained in terms of hydrodynamics. Work in that field has shown us that when a current of water flows along a solid body, the water particles closest to the body are subject to greater retardation than those farther away from the body. When these layers of water (subjected to retardation in varying degrees) flow by one another smoothly, we say that the flow is "laminar." When the difference in speed between them is too great and a whirlpool motion is produced, we say that the flow is "turbulent." A turbulent flow produces much greater resistance than does a laminar flow. The English researchers calculated that the performance of porpoises and dolphins can only be explained by assuming that the water flow along their whole body is laminar.

Understandably enough experiments with models were undertaken in order to ascertain whether the flow is in fact laminar. But these experiments did not produce any satisfactory results because the experimenters were forced to work with rigid models, and the flow along a self-propelling body such as that of a swimming dolphin is quite different from the flow along a rigid body like that of the model. So far we have not succeeded in getting a model that mimics a swimming dolphin. But the experiments have produced certain indications that the flow is indeed laminar.

Because of the much greater length and the bodily form of the rorquals, it is quite possible that the flow along their body is turbulent to some extent at least. It is estimated that one need only assume a turbulent flow along the back third of the larger whale body in order to be able to explain the high resistance and thus correlate their speed with the speed of the dolphins.

We can also try to explain this by interjecting another factor, which in all likelihood works together with the aforementioned one. It would seem that the back muscles and tail muscles of the dolphin, which serve as the main motor of all these animals, are attached to the vertebral processes in a manner superior to those of the large whales. A complete explanation would exceed the limits of this small book. Here we might indicate that because of the position where their tendons are attached to the spinal processes and the chevron bones (located on the lower side of the caudal vertebra), the muscles of the dolphin can operate with a much greater lever arm than those of the great whales.

IV. *Breathing and Diving*

In children's books and on the labels of codliver-oil bottles whales are often depicted with a pretty stream of water spouting from their head. The picture is erroneous, however, because it is not really a stream of water but rather a cloud of steam known as the whale's "blow." Whales are mammals. They breathe with lungs not gills, and hence they are compelled to return to the surface in order to renew the air in their lungs. The characteristic cloud of vapor (Figs. 23, 77) occurs during exhalation. It is three to four meters high in right whales, 2 meters high in humpback whales, four to six meters high in fin whales, six meters high in blue whales, and five to eight meters high in sperm whales. From the form of the blow an expert can usually determine quite well the species in question, especially when there is no strong wind to disperse the blow. Right whales have a double blow, rorquals have a more or less pear-shaped blow (Fig. 24), and sperm whales have a blow aimed diagonally forward (Fig. 25).

It is obvious enough that the whale's blow consists of condensed water vapor. Many people are inclined to assume that this vapor cloud arises in the same way as does the white cloud of breath we see coming from our own mouths on a chilly day. But the fact is that the whale's blow is just as evident in warm waters as it is in icy currents. So we must conclude that the condensation of water vapor occurs mainly through the expansion of

FIG. 23. Three fin whales surfacing. The "blow" of the whale on the left is clearly visible. Photo by W. L. van Utrecht (Amsterdam).

FIG. 24. Vapor cloud of a surfacing sei whale. After Andrews (1916).

FIG. 25. Sketch by J. Stel of a sperm whale off the coast of South America surfacing, blowing, and showing its flukes.

respiratory gases. In other words the air breathed is pressed with enormous force through the relatively narrow nasal duct and the blowhole. In the process the air is greatly compressed. Then it suddenly expands in the open air and is cooled so much that the water it contains is condensed into vapor.

The whole process of breathing in and out lasts only one to two seconds. A quantity of air in the range of 2000 liters can pass through the blowhole of a great whale twice in this short span of time. When rorquals are swimming peacefully on the surface, one usually sees a new blow every one to two minutes; when they dive really deep, the time between breaths can range anywhere from four to forty minutes. Naturally this breathing pause is closely connected with the depth of the dive.

The food of the large rorquals, the "krill," is found mainly in the upper fifty meters of the sea, and especially in the first ten meters below the surface. Hence the whales do not usually dive deeper than ten to fifty meters. But pressure gauges attached to harpoons have established that they can dive to 350 meters without any difficulty. We know that even more fantastic performances can be executed by sperm and bottlenose whales. From the cuttlefish found in the maws of these whales we know that they can dive to a depth of 500 meters at least. The most significant data about the whale's diving depth, however, comes from the carcasses or skeletons of sperm whales who were entangled in some telephone or telegraph cable on the ocean floor and therefore drowned (Fig. 26). We know of thirteen such cases so far. Most of them come from the Pacific coast of North America, but others come from the coast off Brazil and the Persian Gulf. In six cases the cable was located at a depth of 900 meters, in one case at a depth of 988 meters. This means that the animal in question fought for its life at a pressure of 100 atmospheres. In general the large whales are occasionally exposed to a pressure of 40 to 50 atmospheres. By contrast the common porpoise and dolphins apparently do not usually dive more than 25 meters, although Cadenat claims that porpoises off the west coast of Africa (Dakar) can dive as deep as 200 meters. The deepest that an unprotected human being can dive is somewhere around 120 meters.

FIG. 26. Sketches of sperm whales caught in undersea telephone cables, based on descriptions provided by ship captains involved. These incidents took place off the coasts of Peru and Ecuador at a depth of 250 and 290 meters. After Heezen (1957).

People are often inclined to feel that the body of a whale would be completely compressed by being exposed to a pressure of forty to one hundred atmospheres. There is not really much danger of this, however, because most of its body is composed of noncompressible material; only its air-filled lungs represent a basic danger. Since the lung volume can be reduced up to about

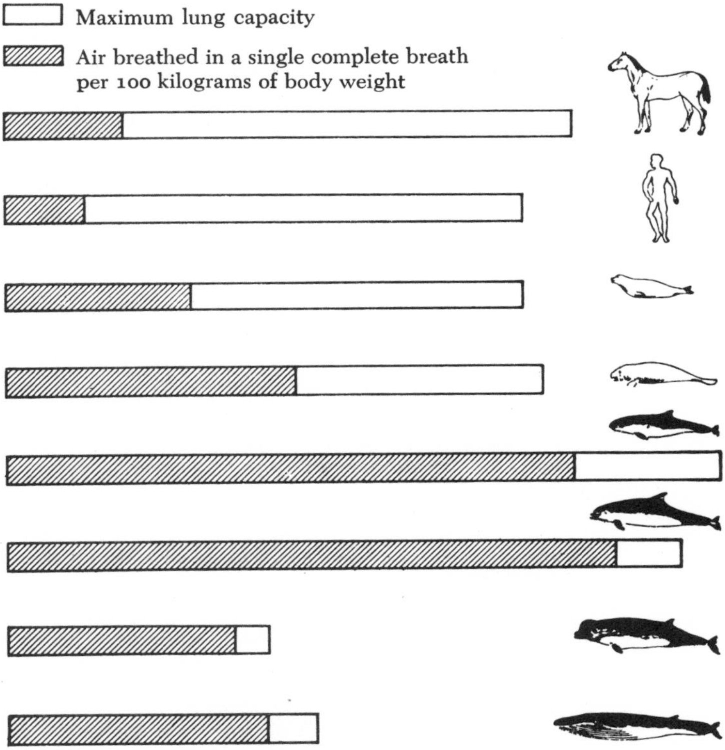

FIG. 27. Chart depicting the maximum amount of air the lungs can hold, and the amount of air breathed in and out with each breath—calculated per 100 kilograms of body weight for a horse, a human being, a seal, a sea cow, a common porpoise, a bottlenose dolphin, a bottlenose whale, and a fin whale. Based on data of Irving and Scholander.

1/10 (Fig. 27), it is only under a depth of 100 meters that a difference in pressure between lung volume and the exterior can show up. The smaller the lung volume or lung content, the fewer the problems posed by this difference in pressure. Thus in deep-diving species it is critically important that they take only a small amount of air with them as they descend. In other words, it is critically important that their lung volume be small in proportion to their body size.

That is actually what happens. In proportion to their size, the weight and maximum capacity of the lungs of sperm whales, bottlenose whales, and rorquals is approximately one half that of land mammals. By contrast the lungs of common porpoises and dolphins, which do not make deep dives, are about one and a half to two times as large—as is the case with their relatives living on land (Fig. 27).

The reader may ask: How is that possible? Sperm whales and bottlenose whales can remain under water from fifty to ninety minutes, fin whales and blue whales can dive for up to forty minutes, although their normal diving time ranges from five to fifteen minutes. How is it possible for them to get by with such a small reserve of oxygen in their lungs when common porpoises and dolphins, with a diving period of five minutes at most, have a relatively larger amount of oxygen in their lungs?

Before we try to answer this question, one point should be stressed. Both in terms of their maximum breathing interval and in terms of breathing frequency, the performance of all whales and dolphins is far superior to that of land mammals. In general, human beings cannot dive for longer than one minute; trained pearl divers can extend the time to about 2½ minutes. Dogs and cats will not survive a breathing pause of three minutes. Breathing frequency is intimately tied up with the absolute size of an animal. The number of breaths per minute is about 100 for rats, 60 for rabbits, 16 for human beings, and 6 for elephants. When we take the diving period into account, then the breathing frequency of rorquals and sperm whales is about 1 breath per 2 minutes (Fig. 28); this can be regarded as normal for animals of that size. On the other hand, a total frequency of one to three breaths per minute for the small dolphins is very small because their weight dovetails with that of human beings in broad outlines.

Now if we ask ourselves why the large whales with their small lungs have proportionally the same breathing rate as land mammals whereas the dolphins have such a low breathing rate, it would be sensible enough to assume that there are other places besides the lungs which maintain an oxygen reserve in the body during a dive,

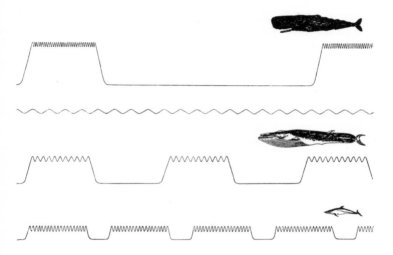

FIG. 28. Schematic picture of breathing frequency of the sperm whale (long diving period and swimming calmly on the surface), the fin whale (dives 10 to 15 minutes), and the dolphin (dives intermittently in a short period of time). Each peak in the graph represents a time of surfacing and blowing.

and that there is a far greater abundance of such places in whales than in land mammals. These places do in fact exist, specifically in the muscles, where a large amount of oxygen can be chemically bound to the red muscle pigment myohemoglobin. The latter possesses just about the same oxygen-combining characteristics as the red blood pigment hemoglobin. When land mammals such as human beings dive, the following oxygen reserves have been established: 34 percent in the lungs, 41 percent in the blood, 13 percent in the muscles, and 12 percent in other tissues. For whales, by contrast, the figures are: 9 percent in the lungs, 41 percent in the blood (the transport medium), 41 percent in the muscles, and 8 percent in other organs. The dark color of whale meat indicates that the myohemoglobin content of the whale's muscles is in fact greater than that in land mammals.

Nevertheless the large oxygen reserve in the muscles does not fully explain the diving performance of whales. We are forced to assume that the process of metabolism in the muscles during a dive takes place differently than it does during the time when a whale is above the surface. It is very likely that during a dive there occurs only a partial oxidative process, i.e., a combustion process without free oxygen. The complete oxidation would then occur when the animal is on the surface.

The small lung capacity of deep-diving whales also explains why they do not suffer from such diving problems as the bends (caisson disease). The amount of air in their lungs is so small in proportion to their size that only a very small quantity of air is dissolved in the blood and it does not form nitrogen bubbles in the process of surfacing. The amount of air available to human beings is very great because new air is constantly added.

Because the breathing rate of cetaceans is so low, practically the whole content of the lungs must be renewed with each breath. Figure 27 shows that this is not the case with human beings and other land mammals, in which the volume of air in a single inhalation and exhalation amounts to only 10 to 15 percent of the maximum lung capacity. The cetaceans take in 85 to 90 percent of this maximum capacity in a single exhalation and inhalation. Thus they must breathe much more deeply because they breathe more slowly.

As we have already noted, cetacean air passages are relatively narrow. For this reason, particularly in the case of the dolphins which have large lungs, significant fluctuations in pressure occur through the whole respiratory apparatus. These fluctuations impose very strict demands on the tissue structure of these organs. One can also expect such sharp fluctuations in pressure when a cetacean dives or surfaces, and this is particularly true in the case of the deep-diving species. So we should not be surprised to find various structural adaptations to pressure fluctuations in the lungs, the trachea, the pharynx, and the nose.

In all land mammals the trachea and the large bronchii are covered with cartilaginous rings so that they will remain open during air intake, as illustrated on the tube of a vacuum cleaner. In the case of the cetaceans this cartilaginous covering is found not only in the trachea and the large bronchii but also in the minutest branches of the bronchial tree (Fig. 29). This permits a quick flow through and ensures that most sections of the air passages cannot be compressed. Elastic fibers are not found just in the wall of the bronchii and in the remaining lung tissues, they are also found specifically in the outer covering of the lungs, the pleura, thus giving a yellow and wrinkled appearance to the lungs of large whales. The great elasticity ensures prompt and smooth adaptation to pressure fluctuations.

Another adaptation is the noteworthy system of valves that is found in the bronchioles of dolphins. We find a system of 25 to 40 folds of mucous membrane lying one

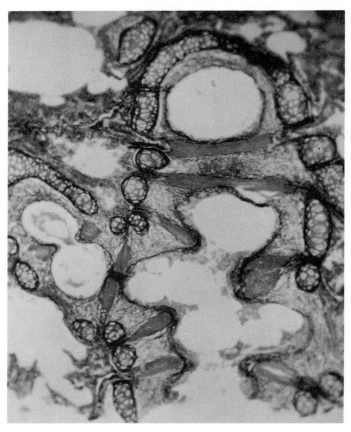

FIG. 29. Microscopic picture of a longitudinal section through a small bronchiole (*Bronchiolus respiratorius*) in the lung of a bottlenose dolphin. One can see the protuberances, fitted out with circular muscles, which form the interconnected series of valves. One can also see the cartilaginous covering of this bronchiole. Photo by W. L. van Utrecht (Amsterdam).

behind the other and protruding into the lumen of the bronchii. In these folds are circularly arranged muscle fibers which can close the lumen completely when they contract (Fig. 29). When the muscles are relaxed, the lumen is kept open by elastic fibers running radially to the cartilaginous covering. The whole check valve ensures that during a dive air cannot be pressed from the soft pulmonary alveoli into the rigid bronchial system. Any technician experienced in working with great differences in pressure will tell you that you do not use a single stopcock in such cases. Instead you use a series of valves arranged one behind the other so that the pressure differences can be balanced out smoothly. We do not find this valve system in the bronchioles of deep-diving whales (e.g., baleen whales, sperm whales, and bottle-nose whales) but in their bodies not only every alveolar passage but also every single pulmonary vesicle can be closed by a circular muscle.

The small porpoises and dolphins have a relatively large lung capacity, and they have more specialized adaptations to pressure fluctuations in the respiratory apparatus than do the deep-diving whales with their relatively smaller lung capacity. This fact is reflected in the structure of the larynx and the blowhole. Bartholinus noted the peculiar shape of the common porpoise's larynx back in 1654 (*Historiarum anatomicarum rariorum*), remarking that it looked like the head of a goose. He was the first to point out the laryngeal feature that is characteristic of all the Odontoceti: two cartilages of the larynx, the epiglottis, and the arytenoid cartilage are elongated so that they look like the beak of a goose. This produces a tube-shaped elongation of the larynx which protrudes into the lower portion of the nasal duct (Fig. 30). This "goose-beak" is surrounded by the circular musculature of the pharynx; it can be closed by this musculature and hence operates like a valve.

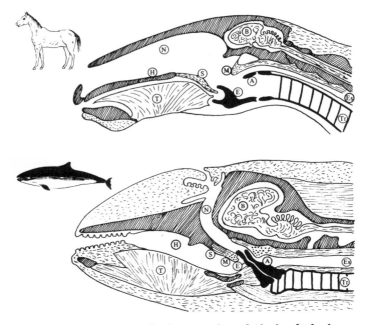

FIG. 30. Schematic longitudinal section through the head of a horse and the head of a porpoise to show the position of the nasal duct and the structure of the pharynx and larynx. N: nasal duct; H: hard palate; S: soft palate; M: circular muscle surrounding the beak of the larynx; T: tongue; E: epiglottis; A: arytenoid cartilage; Tr: trachea; Es: esophagus; B: brain. Partially based on Rawitz (1900).

The operation of this valve is in turn supported by the operation of distinctive protuberances in the blowhole. Anyone who has tried to put his arm into the blowhole of a dead whale knows that he must use a great deal of energy to overcome the resistance of the closed lips. Even then the blowhole is passively closed by highly developed, elastic tissue. It is opened by the contraction of a radially arranged muscle, whose fibers extend from the lips of the blowhole toward the skull bone. Underneath the opening of the blowhole in toothed whales is a system of protuberances from the nasal duct, which are often greatly ramified. Together with the goose-shaped beak of the larynx they form a system of serried valves and interrelated air pockets. Among other things, they permit the animal to emit a precisely measured dose of air through the blowhole when it is under water, as is the case when they emit vocalizations under water (see chapter 7).

In baleen whales we do not find a goose-shaped larynx jutting into the pharynx nor do we find the system of protuberances in the blowhole. However, we do find a large sack-shaped protuberance on the bottom side of the larynx, but the functional significance of this noteworthy organ is as yet unknown.

v. Blood Circulation

When President Eisenhower had a heart attack in 1955, an immediate call went out to Doctor Paul Dudley White of Boston who was the most noted heart specialist in the United States. White's vast experience, however, was not confined to heart conditions among the notables of human society. He had long been trying to unlock the cardiac secrets of the largest and most powerful beasts in the animal kingdom. Using electrocardiographs, he had already explored the heart of an elephant; and for many years he had been trying to get an electrocardiogram of a great whale.

He had managed to do this with a beluga, the white whale that inhabits the Arctic waters. In Bristol Bay (Alaska) electrode-tipped harpoons were shot into a white whale measuring four meters in length. For about a half hour Doctor White registered this whale's heartbeat. In January 1957 he repeated the experiment with a gray whale in the California lagoon. It seemed dangerous to approach the whale in a motor boat, so the experiment was conducted from a helicopter. But this experiment was unsuccessful because the whale was too disturbed by the air currents.

In the white whale Doctor White found a heart rate, a pulse of about 16 to 17 beats per minute. This seemed a surprisingly low count for an animal weighing 1136 kilograms, when we consider that elephants have a pulse of about 30 and that the heartbeat of an animal is more or

51

less inversely proportional to its absolute size. A horse
has a pulse of 40 beats per minute, a human being has a
pulse of 70, a cat has a pulse of 150, and a mouse has a
pulse of 650. We know that when human beings and
other land mammals dive under water, the rate is only
about half of that above the water. In this respect, then,
a pulse of 17 in a white whale is nothing special. The same
can be said of the heartbeat of a porpoise, whose pulse
was recorded by Irving at 50 under water and 110 above
the surface in Marineland Aquarium (Florida).

On 5 December 1959 a live fin whale, 15 meters long,
was stranded on Cape Cod and lived for twenty-four
hours. J. Kanwisher of the Woods Hole Oceanographic
Institute found a pulse of 25 in the animal (Fig. 31). But
since the animal was breathing at three times the normal
rate, we should probably assume a normal pulse of 8
beats per minute above the surface and 4 beats per minute beneath the surface. That is exactly the rate which
Pütter calculated for such a large whale in 1924. All
these findings indicate that the heart rate of cetaceans
does not show any special adaptation to their aquatic
mode of life.

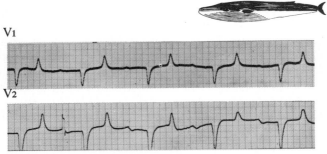

FIG. 31. Cardiogram of a fin whale, 15 meters long, stranded on
Cape Cod in December 1959. Taken by J. Kanwisher (Woods
Hole).

The same conclusion results from studies of the weight of their heart, its overall form and internal architecture (Fig. 32), and the distribution of elastic tissue in their arterial system. Neither the heart nor the large blood vessels give the slightest indication of doing anything special to adapt to the whale's aquatic mode of life or its diving habits. Nor does the total quantity of blood as compared with bodily size and stature diverge the slightest from the ratio found in land mammals.

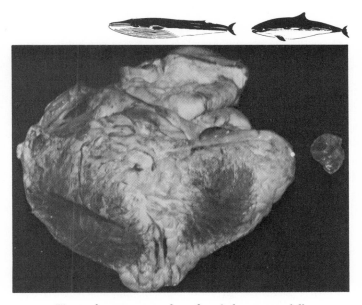

FIG. 32. Heart of a 15.5 meter long fin whale, not yet fully grown, alongside the heart of a common porpoise. The latter's heart is about the same size as that of a human being. Note the shape of the heart (very broad), which is determined by the volume ratio in the thorax. Photo by W. L. van Utrecht (Amsterdam).

Nevertheless at certain points in the circulatory system we do find noteworthy structures which are indisputably tied up with the whale's aquatic life. First of all there are the *retia mirabilia* ("wonder-nets"). If we dissect a common porpoise or a dolphin, we will find a thick spongy mass on the back side of the thorax along the vertebral column. One gets the impression that this mass holds a great deal of blood. We note that this mass extends into the throat and, to some extent, between the ribs. These networks were noted by anatomists in the seventeenth and eighteenth century, e.g., Tyson (1680) and Monro (1787). The first thorough description was provided by Breschet (1836), who even then had a perfectly clear idea of the more detailed anatomy of this organ (Fig. 33).

The *retia mirabilia* are composed of small arteries branching out in every direction. They wind around each other in tangled patterns and can intercommunicate. Through capillaries these small arteries pass over into an equally tangled web of small efferent veins. The whole mass is imbedded in a matrix of connective tissue containing lymphatic vessels and numerous fat cells. (Fig. 34). The arteries feeding into this network have elastic walls, but the walls of the arteries in the network itself consist almost completely of muscular tissue (Fig. 34). This fact and the highly sinuous course of the vessels suggest that here we have a portion of the vascular system which can display very great fluctuations in volume and is therefore in a position to compensate for great fluctuations in blood pressure. Here the veins, the lymphatic vessels, and the fat cells, in particular, can play the role of shock absorbers. *Retia mirabilia* are also found in other sections of the whale's body—particularly in the vertebral canal, at the base of the brain, and on the outer side of the base of the skull.

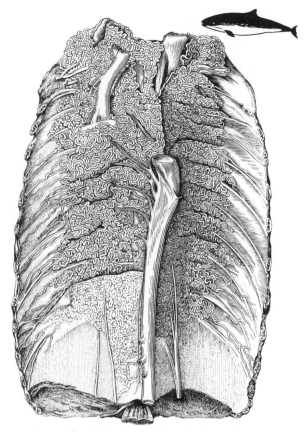

FIG. 33. Inner side of the thorax (dorsal side) of a common porpoise, with its *rete mirabile*. The aorta and the outlet section of the veins in the vertebral canal (left) can also be seen. After a copper engraving by Breschet (1836).

By contrast somewhat divergent structures are evident in the *retia mirabilia* which are found mainly on the back side of the abdominal cavity. They consist solely of inter-

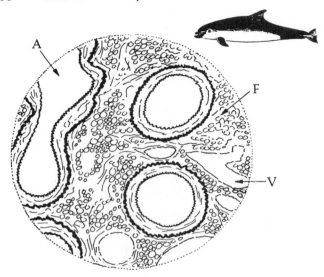

FIG. 34. Microscope cross section through the *rete mirabile* in the thoracic wall of a bottlenose dolphin. A: artery; V: vein; F: fat cells.

connected veins. They receive blood chiefly from the collateral caudal veins, while the blood flows off toward the inferior vena cava or the longitudinal veins of the vertebral canal.

The longitudinal veins are two relatively spacious vessels which lie on the lower side of the spinal cord and traverse the whole vertebral canal from the ventricle of the brain to the end of the tail. They form the outlet for blood coming from the brain and, with the help of numerous lateral veins, are connected with both the anterior and the posterior vena cava. The fact that these vessels have the same diameter for the entire length, as well as the absence of valves, readily leads us to conjecture that the blood in these longitudinal veins can flow in either direction.

In addition to the arterial *retia mirabilia,* the venous *retia mirabilia,* and the longitudinal veins in the vertebral canal, we find a fourth cetacean adaptation to aquatic life in the toothed whales. They display a sinuslike enlargement of the hepatic veins and of that section of the inferior vena cava into which these veins discharge. What is more, this vena cava can be closed off by a circular muscle as it passes through the mediastinum. Many of the formations described here can also be found in other aquatic mammals, but they are usually less pronounced than in the cetaceans.

The most surprising fact is that among the cetaceans these features are best developed in porpoises, somewhat less developed in common and bottlenose dolphins, and least developed in the large, deep-diving whales. Hence they certainly are not adaptations to residence in the lower depths of the sea. We are led to assume that here, just as in the case of features peculiar to the respiratory organs, we are dealing with adaptations to fluctuations in pressure. It is obvious that sharp fluctuations in pressure can occur in the vascular system of a diving or surfacing whale. The point is made clear to us when we picture a thirty-meter-long blue whale in a vertical dive and realize that between the tip of its snout and its flukes the difference in pressure—and hence in blood pressure—is three atmospheres.

But large pressure fluctuations can also occur in the circulatory system during heavy breathing. We can experience this sort of fluctuation in blood pressure if we try to exhale with our mouth and nose closed off. This phenomenon, known as the Valsalva effect, occurs with every exhalation of the whale; and pressure differences during inhalation also have a reaction on the circulatory

system. We can readily picture the operation of the aforementioned apparatuses if we take a hypothetical example. Suppose that the pressure in the thoracic cavity is
greater momentarily than that in the abdominal cavity.
The blood is then temporarily stored in the venous *retia
mirabilia* and in the enlarged hepatic veins, while the circular muscle of the mediastinum prevents blood from
running back from the heart. Blood from the brain can
flow down to the abdominal cavity. On the other hand
when the blood pressure in the thoracic cavity is lower
than elsewhere in the body, a great deal of blood is sucked
into the cavity. The heart must pump this blood through
the rest of the body, overcoming considerable resistance
in the process. This resistance can be overcome, in part,
through the enlargement of the *retia mirabilia* in the
thoracic cavity.

It is very possible that all these fluctuations in blood
pressure play a more significant role in porpoises and
dolphins than they do in the larger, deep-diving whales.
For porpoises and dolphins have relatively larger lungs,
and they breathe and dive more frequently.

We cannot close our discussion of blood circulation
without saying a few words about the blood itself. The
blood of the whale has been studied often in the hope of
gaining a better insight into the diving mode of life. But
all such studies have merely shown that the oxygen-
combining capability of the hemoglobin is exactly the
same as that in land mammals. If the red blood pigment
of whales bound oxygen more readily, the emission of
oxygen into the tissues would be more difficult and
thereby retard the replenishment of oxygen reserves during breathing.

In the case of animals who spend only a short time
on the surface of the water, it is very important that this
process be allowed to run its course as quickly as possible. In only one essential feature does the blood of ceta-

ceans differ from that of land mammals: the total volume, and specifically the total surface of the red blood corpuscles is about 1½ to 2 times as great as that of land mammals. This permits both a rapid absorption and a rapid emission of oxygen, i.e., rapid transport.

vi. *Behavior*

As early as the nineteenth century sporadic attempts were made to keep dolphins in captivity. A classic case is the extremely tame bottlenose dolphin whose breathing was studied by Jolyet in 1873 at the Biological Station in Arcachon. In 1877 and again in 1878 the Westminster Aquarium in London played host to a white whale brought over from America. In Brighton and Copenhagen porpoises were put on display, and in 1907 the New York Aquarium possessed a herd of twelve bottlenose dolphins. But all these animals lived for only a few months in captivity.

The Marineland Aquarium in Florida, built just before World War II, was the first installation with a policy of not only keeping dolphins in captivity but also breeding them. Its residents include the bottlenose dolphin, the pilot whale, the spotted dolphin, and even a pigmy sperm whale. This aquarium has two large tanks. One is 30 by 13 meters, and 4 meters deep; the other is a round tank 6 meters deep, with a diameter of 25 meters. Side passages enable spectators to view the animals through glass windows even when they are under water.

Usually these animals are captured with nets. Foam-rubber mattresses are used to prevent injuries during transport. While the animals are out of water, they must be sprinkled with cold water constantly to prevent overheating and skin peeling. Bottlenose dolphins can be picked up out of the water without any trouble, but porpoises will often go into shock at this point and die as a

61

result. Dudok van Heel discovered this for himself in 1958 when he was trying to transport twenty porpoises captured in Denmark. Only a few survived the truck trip to the oceanographic institute at den Helder, and only one lived long enough to have its hearing acuity studied by scientists.

The dolphin and porpoise show at the Florida Marineland Aquarium has been an enormous success. The public has flocked to see these animals, and rival aquariums soon sprang up. Today there are similar installations in the Bahamas, Silver Springs, California (Fig. 35), Australia (in Sydney and Brisbane), and Japan (near Enoshima). In Italy there is a small aquarium near Cesenatico with two bottlenose dolphins. In 1958 Monaco had

FIG. 35. Feeding an old female bottlenose dolphin at the California Marineland Aquarium.

FIG. 36. Bottlenose dolphins being fed under water at the Florida Marineland Aquarium. Photo by F. S. Essapian (Miami).

three dolphins, but their upkeep proved to be too expensive. These animals were tested on their sense of hearing, but practically all other scientific work on cetaceans in captivity comes from the Florida Marineland Aquarium and the California Marineland Aquarium.

Both the possibility of experimentation and its popularity rest first and foremost on the fact that these animals become very tame in short order (Fig. 36). Dudok van

Heel was able to feed his porpoises by hand after only a few days. The common and bottlenose dolphins of the large aquariums let humans pet them with visible relish. Even when they are living free, these animals may develop friendships with human beings. At Opononi Beach (near Auckland in New Zealand) a famous bottlenose dolphin died not long ago. For a year it had been the playmate of visitors to the seashore. It let children ride on its back and took part in games of catching a beach ball. This absence of timidity is common to almost all cetaceans. The large baleen whales and sperm whales will let a human get as close as 25 meters, and they themselves will often swim around a ship with great curiosity. This attitude and behavior seems to be based on the fact that these animals have so few enemies and, as a group, are not threatened by a single natural enemy from above the surface of the water.

The greatest success of these animals is undoubtedly the fact that they can easily be trained to perform all sorts of circus stunts. They can be trained to ring a bell (Fig. 37), to blow a trumpet, to fetch objects, to play ball (Fig. 38), to leap through a tire (Fig. 39), and to tow a boat with a girl and a dog in it. The possibility of teaching them all these tricks is undoubtedly based on their inherent natural playfulness. Playful games and motions can be observed among all cetaceans in the wild. Dolphins and porpoises leap over the water regularly, and the same behavior is evident among such large whales as the humpback whale and the sperm whale (Fig. 18).

In aquariums, bottlenose and common dolphins do not confine their play to members of their own species. They will play with other animals living in the tank, such as turtles and birds (Fig. 40). They will also spend hours playing with pieces of wood, feathers, rubber balls, and inflated tires. Captain Mörzer Bruins has observed wild

FIG. 37. Flippy, the trained bottlenose dolphin, rings the dinner bell at the Florida Marineland Aquarium. After Dillin (1952).

dolphins engaged in a game of diving with cormorants on the Bahrein reefs.

The trainability of these animals is also based on the fact that they are diurnal animals whose active periods roughly coincide with those of human beings over a twenty-four-hour span. They sleep for about an hour after each meal, floating on the surface or not far below it. At night they sleep continuously for long periods. Pilot whales seem to be nocturnal animals, perhaps because they feed on cuttlefish. In any case they sleep the whole day when they are first taken into captivity, and then gradually adapt to the human way of living. Right whales and humpback whales have also been observed sleeping on the surface of the water. But the champion sleeper is certainly the sperm whale, which has been hit by ships occasionally both during the day and during the night.

The trainability of dolphins is also enhanced by the fact that they are carnivores; fish eaters specifically. As such they possess an overall repertoire of behavior patterns that exceeds the repertoire of plant-eating animals, and they are much more receptive to being rewarded with a prize of food. They are also gregarious animals, more closely attached to the human species than to other species that live a solitary life. Up to a certain point they will readily incorporate human beings into their herds.

FIG. 38. Young bottlenose dolphins playing basketball at the California Marineland Aquarium. Photo by D. H. Brown.

FIG. 39. Flippy (see Fig. 37) leaps through a tire with paper stretched across it. Teaching a dolphin to leap into a visually occluded space is no easy matter. After Hill (1957).

Most of the kinds of social units have been found among the cetaceans that are evident among land mammals. Troups of one hundred to one thousand animals of both sexes and of every age have been found among the fin whale, the bottlenose whale, the pilot whale, and many dolphins (e.g., the common dolphin and the bottlenose dolphin). Other species live in smaller herds (ten to twenty animals) of the same composition. Within these herds it seems that unlimited promiscuity prevails. The presence of leaders has never been observed except in the case of the pilot whale and the bottlenose whale; in the latter cases it seemed that the herds were led by an old male. Separate herds of males and females, akin to those found among wild sheep and many species of deer, are also found among some cetaceans: the white whale, the killer whale, and perhaps also the common porpoise. By contrast a close family pattern of living (i.e., male,

FIG. 40. A bottlenose dolphin at the Florida Marineland Aquarium plays with a turtle. Photo by F. S. Essapian (Miami).

female, and one or two young) is led by the blue whale, often by the sei whale, and apparently by the pigmy sperm. On the other hand the large sperm whale, like the sea lion and the baboon, lives in a harem-type of organization. Troups of females with calves and older youngsters are under the leadership of a single adult bull. During the mating season there is a ferocious struggle over this position. The harems remain in warm waters, the rest of the males form troops of varying size and withdraw to polar waters. Loners, who have been driven out of these bands, can be very dangerous to human beings.

Behavioral studies of bottlenose dolphins at the Florida Marineland Aquarium have indicated that there is a very definite social hierarchy among these animals. The fight for rank is carried on with smacks of the tail, head butting, threatening postures and gestures, and jaw snapping. Usually these confrontations are harmless, but sometimes a real fight takes place and severe bite wounds result. As is true in the case of fowl, all males are superior to females. But if there are only females and juveniles in the herd, then hierarchy depends mainly on size and age.

Among the cetaceans mutual ties within the herd are generally very close, and they are apparently maintained primarily by calls. Thus most cetaceans are almost constantly emitting calls, it seems, as is true of many apes and parrots (see chapter 7). Mutual cooperation in the hunt is known to be a sure fact for the killer whale. In large groups they will hunt herds of seals, sea lions, and walruses, circling around them and splitting them up so that they can get at the young of their prey which are usually in the center of the herd.

First aid and assistance to sick or wounded members of the species has been observed among some whales. Most land mammals will abandon the sick and wounded, or even kill them. But some cetaceans, like African elephants, will tend the wounded. At least three times bottlenose dolphins in captivity have been observed doing this. Two of them will support an unconscious companion in the tank so that it can breathe over the surface of the water (Fig. 41). They will shove their own heads under the flippers of the unconscious beast and lift it, but now and then they must abandon this position because they themselves cannot breathe from it. First aid to wounded members of the species has also been observed among bottlenose dolphins, humpback whales, and gray whales. Sperm whales will come from great distances when a

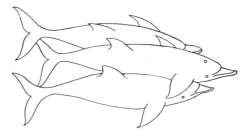

ꜰɪɢ. 41. Two bottlenose dolphins support an injured comrade keeping its nostril above water. After Siebenaler and Caldwell (1956).

herd member is injured. The common porpoise and several other dolphin species behave differently; they are frightened off by the calls of wounded companions.

Sperm whales appear to carry their wounded young with their jaws above the water. Bottlenose dolphins have been observed to do similar things with dead or dismembered young who fell prey to sharks or barracudas. The mother will periodically push the carcass or parts of it upward toward the surface over the period of a whole day. Apparently this behavior pattern of shoving things up to the surface is triggered in these animals by any object that is not moving on its own in the water. In the Marineland Aquarium bottlenose dolphins have often been seen to push tubes, pieces of wood, and even small sharks in this way. On the open sea, sperm whales have been observed doing the same thing with wooden beams and logs. It is quite possible that this behavior pattern is the basis for the legend of Arion's rescue by a dolphin and for similar tales of desperate humans being rescued by dolphins. There is a very recent and well-documented account of a woman who was drowning off the coast of Florida and who was pushed to shore by a bottlenose dolphin.

VII. *Orientation and Communication*

For most mammals living on land, the most important sense for orientation in the environment is the sense of smell. Smelling—i.e., the perception of olfactory chemical stimuli—is very feasible in water. Fish, for example, have a well developed olfactory organ. But when particles are dissolved or released in water, land mammals perceive them with their taste organs. Only particles in air are perceived by their olfactory organs.

Cetaceans do not have to absorb any sensory impressions from the air. And once they had shifted to aquatic life, the olfactory organ could not be restructured to perceive particles released in the water.[1] Thus the organ of smell lost its functional importance and atrophied completely. Baleen whales still retain a small vestige of the olfactory mucuous membrane and the olfactory nerve, but no trace of an olfactory apparatus remains in the brain of toothed whales.

To the best of our knowledge at present, this reduction of the olfactory organ has not been compensated for by the development of some other organ for chemical perception or by the stronger development of the gustatory sense. Taste organs seem to be totally absent in the baleen whales, and they are poorly developed in the

---

1. Evolutionary studies have indicated this general result: once an organ has been restructured, it does not return in its original form to its original function.

toothed whales. This should not surprise us too much because all the cetaceans are carnivores which generally gulp down their prey. They, unlike herbivores, are not in great danger of taking in poisonous particles with their food.

As yet we know very little about their sense of touch, but certain features of their cerebellum suggest a well-developed tactile sense. When live whales and dolphins have been stranded on a beach, it has been observed that they react to the slightest touching of their hide. In captivity bottlenose and common dolphins are delighted with petting, and they enjoy rubbing themselves on coarse objects in the tank (Fig. 42). The tactile hairs of the

FIG. 42. A bottlenose dolphin at the Florida Marineland Aquarium rubs itself on the head of a street-cleaner's broom. Photo by F. S. Essapian (Miami).

baleen whales and the cushion of connective tissue on the
snout of many toothed whales may be particularly sensitive to water pressure or water current. But we have not
yet investigated their importance for orientation, so we
must exclude them from any further consideration here
in our discussion of the sensory life of cetaceans.

At a depth of thirty-five meters in the North Sea, 98
percent of the light is extinguished. What is more, light
reflected off objects under water penetrates only a distance of seventeen meters, so that a large blue whale cannot even see its own flukes. Considering these facts it is
readily apparent that under water the eye cannot be of
great importance for long-range orientation. For close-
range orientation the sense of sight does play a real role.
Observation of the bottlenose dolphins in the Marineland Aquarium has established that they use their eyes
to pursue and capture their prey. This seems to be the
case with all dolphins and porpoises which feed on extremely mobile prey (i.e., fish). Pilot whales and sperm
whales feed on cuttlefish, and baleen whales feed on
plankton; eyes are of little importance in their case, and
they are accordingly much smaller. The Ganges dolphin
in fact, which hunts its prey in the muddy river bottom,
is totally blind; its atrophied eyes lack a lens.

In terms of the structure and function of their eyes,
certain special demands are imposed on whales for seeing under water. Light reflection in water is different from
light refraction in air. When we find ourselves under
water, the image of a perceived object falls behind our
retina. We become far-sighted and are forced to correct
the haziness of the image by adapting our lens or using
glasses with convex lenses. Whales have already adjusted
to this situation. They have globular lenses which produce the same effect as the convex lenses just mentioned.
This means that they are short-sighted in the air, however, and must therefore make some accommodation to

correct the situation (Fig. 43). The accommodating muscles in question have been found in toothed whales; they seem to be absent in baleen whales. Studies of bottlenose dolphins in various aquariums have shown that these animals can perceive accurately above water up to a distance of fifteen meters. One white-sided dolphin at the Florida Marineland Aquarium had the habit of surfacing with pebbles from the bottom of the tank and

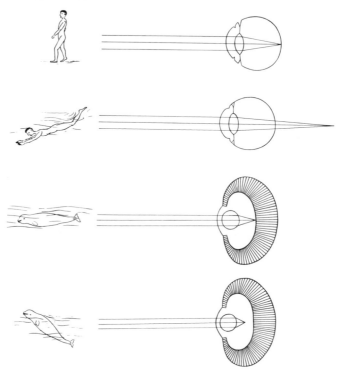

FIG. 43. Path of rays and point of image in the eye of a human being and a white whale in water and in the open air. Note the thickness of the sclera in the whale.

throwing them at the public. The fact that his favorite targets were black-garbed clergymen indicated that he could aim well and that his perception was quite keen.

Another adaptation of the cetacean eye to aquatic life is to be found in the great thickness of the fibrous sclera (Fig. 43). This cannot be regarded as a protection against compression because the whole substance of the eye is noncompressible. Its function is to maintain the oval shape of the eye, which otherwise would turn globular from the water pressure on all sides. Like many twilight animals, whales possess another special adaptation to the weak intensity of light under water. They have a well-developed tapetum, which is an iridescent layer behind the retina. It reflects light and sends it back through the retina a second time. The better developed rods in the retina also seem to be connected with the dim lighting of their milieu.

It should not surprise us that these aquatic animals lack a lachrymal gland, but they do have protection from the effects of salt water on their eyes. The outer layers of the cornea are really horny, and their Harderian gland secretes an oily substance which protects their eyes.

As we have indicated, smell and other chemical senses are almost wholly absent in the cetaceans; what is more, the sense of sight plays only a limited role for closeup orientation. It is not surprising, then, that their hearing organ plays an essential role for long-distance orientation and for communication. Even in antiquity it was known that these animals possess good hearing. Pindar tells us how dolphins can be attracted by music, and Aristotle wondered over the fact that they could be hunted with noise-making objects even though it seemed to him that they did not possess an auditory canal. Later studies have shown that they do possess an auditory canal even though they do not display any external ear. Their auditory canal takes the form of a thin tube filled with sea-water; in baleen whales part of the canal is closed and has been transformed into a web of connective tissue.

Any whaler will tell you that the great whales are very sensitive to noises. Prior to World War II, when we did not possess such fast catcher boats as we do now, we had to sneak up on whales. Catcher boats with nonoscillating steam engines were used for this purpose. Today we use boats with internal combustion engines which make a lot of noise, and overtake the whales as they flee. In ancient Japan whaling was carried on with nets, and hunters beat the water to drive the whales into their trap. The same method is still used for hunting the common porpoise in Denmark and for hunting other kinds of dolphins.

The behavior of dolphins in captivity has made it possible to experiment with them and to determine such things as their range of hearing. Training experiments with bottlenose dolphins have shown that they respond to tones between 150 and 153,000 cycles per second. But their reaction drops markedly in intensity above 120,000 cycles per second. Cycles per second (cps) is a measure of pitch and indicates the number of vibrations per second. Our normal counterpart is around 350 cycles per second. The upper hearing limit for human beings lies between 15,000 and 20,000 cycles per second; we cannot hear tones above that. A cat can react to tones as high as 50,000 cps. For rats the figure is 90,000 cps, and for bats it is 175,000 cps. All the tones which we cannot hear are called "supersonic." Thus a considerable portion of the tones perceptible to cetaceans lie in the supersonic range. The great whales will often react quite noticeably to the supersonic tones of a sonic depth finder or an anti-submarine detection device.

The advantage of high tones for hearing under water is that the vibration cone is less dispersed and hence has a higher capacity for penetration. Schevill and Lawrence have experimented on bottlenose dolphins and have shown that at a distance of 25 meters under water these dolphins are quite capable of ascertaining the direction of calls. The studies of Dudok van Heel on common porpoises have shown that the directional hearing of these animals under water is just as acute as man's directional hearing in the open air.

Obviously enough, well-developed directional hearing is one of the essential requirements that must be met by the most important organ for cetacean orientation. It is remarkable, therefore, that all those who investigated the hearing organ of whales and dolphins—from Claudius (1858) to Yamada (1953)—repeatedly affirmed that the vibrations from the water to the inner ear have transmitted through the bone. Yet in bone conduction, where the whole skull vibrates as well, it is not possible for the vibrations to reach the left and right hearing organ with any noticeable difference in time, intensity, or phase; and directional hearing is grounded on precisely this difference.

Directional hearing is possible only when the left and right hearing organs are acoustically isolated: that is, when they are separated by a medium that propagates the vibrations only minimally if at all. In the case of land-based mammals this is made possible by the isolation of the two tympanic membranes, while the vibrations in the air are almost completely erased when they reach the bones. In water, where this is not the case, directional hearing is almost impossible for human beings. In the case of aquatic animals, then, there must be some other sort of isolation for the left and right hearing organs. Fraser and Purves (1954) and Reysenbach de Haan (1955) made a signal contribution when they showed us how this isolation comes about in the cetaceans.

The vibrations in the water are conducted through the strandlike outer auditory canal to the tympanic membrane. Through the auditory ossicle in the tympanic cavity (the middle ear) they are then transmitted to the inner ear where they are perceived by the sensory epithelium. The tympanic cavity is located in the interior of a very special bone on the bottom of the skull, known as the Tympano-petro-mastoid bone. For the sake of convenience we shall call it the "bone of the middle ear" (Fig. 44). Now on this same bone there is also a shell-shaped protrusion of hard, glasslike bony tissue: the *bulla tympani.* In the bulla we find a bubblelike protrusion of the tympanic cavity. The whole bone of the middle ear is very firmly attached to the rest of the skull. What is more, it is surrounded by a thick layer of foam-filled air spaces (these being bubblelike protrusions of the tympanic cavity also). It is precisely this foamy mass that ensures the acoustic isolation of the middle ear from the

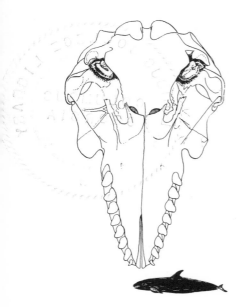

FIG. 44. Skull bottom of a false killer whale showing the position of the *bulla.* After van Beneden and Gervais (1880).

rest of the skull bone. Thus the vibrations of the tympanic membrane can only be transmitted from the auditory ossicle to the inner ear.

The auditory ossicle is so constructed that it has small mass and great tension. By comparing this format with that of violin strings we realize that these features are particularly suited to the propagation of high tones. Back in 1908 a Viennese researcher, W. Kolmer, visited the Zoological Station at St. Andrews in Scotland. Through his histological study of the inner ear of a common porpoise he ascertained that there are very special cells in the membrane where the oscillations are perceived, and that these same kind of cells are also found in other mammals who are capable of hearing high tones (e.g., bats). The two most important adaptations of the auditory canal in cetaceans then are: (1) isolation of the left and right auditory canal (for directional hearing); (2) perception of high tones.

From what has been said so far we would expect that these animals are primarily dependent on vocalizations for intercommunication. We would also expect to find that at least some of these vocalizations are in the supersonic range. This setup not only has the technical and acoustic advantage mentioned above but also ensures that their calls will not be confused with those emitted by fishes and other inhabitants of the sea. The sounds of sea fish lie in a range between 100 and 1500 cycles per second, their optimum strength being around 350 cycles per second. Some crustaceans emit tones between 1000 and 25,000 cycles per second. Thus most of the supersonic calls emitted by cetaceans lie outside the frequency range of other denizens of the sea, and the animals do not disturb each other.

Since the time of Aristotle man has been aware of calls emitted by whales and dolphins above the surface of the water. The normal exhalation of large whales produces a vibrating, whistling call that can be perceived over great distances. For a long time men have known that the white whale produces sounds under water that can be heard above the surface. In the eighteenth century English whalers dubbed this animal the "sea canary," and an old Russian expression talks about "screaming like a white whale."

Using an underwater microphone (a hydrophone) in the open sea and in aquariums, people have picked up a whole series of calls from bottlenose dolphins, common dolphins, pilot whales, and white whales; and they have managed to record them (Fig. 45). Usually it is a whistling tone ranging between 7000 and 15,000 cycles per

FIG. 45. Two bottlenose dolphins hovering around a hydrophone at the Florida Marineland Aquarium. Photo by F. S. Essapian (Miami).

second in the case of the bottlenose dolphin, and between 500 and 10,000 cycles per second in the case of the white whale. This tone regularly accompanies the emission of air bubbles from the blowhole. People have noticed that this is a means of communication among the animals. When the animals are provoked by something, or when a young calf has been separated from its mother, the number of tones increases sharply.

Forceful claps of the jaws are a means of intimidation designed to maintain the proper social hierarchy (see chapter 6). Barking and mewing sounds have been noted at eating time, and a kind of whimpering has been heard during mating. Chiming sounds, smacking, moaning and belching have also been noted. Some researchers also believe that they have heard calls coming from the large whales, but the many attempts to record these calls have proved to be unsuccessful so far. Yet it would be foolish to assume that there is no underwater sound contact between animals who have such well-developed hearing organs. Improved equipment should ensure successful recording some day in the future. (This has, in fact, been accomplished since the original appeared, in 1962.)

Our phonograph recordings of cetacean calls obviously deal with calls whose pitch is below 20,000 cycles per second. But the latest and most up-to-date equipment is able to pick up tones as high as 200,000 cycles per second, and we have established that a considerable portion of cetacean vocalizations are in the supersonic range. When we consider the fact that cetaceans can produce and pick up very high tones, and that they do not possess any other sensory organ for long-distance orientation under water, then we may quite naturally deduce that they use some sort of radar system to orient themselves under water—just as bats do in the dark. It would be something akin to a sonar device or a submarine-detection device. Like these it would send out very high frequency vibrations

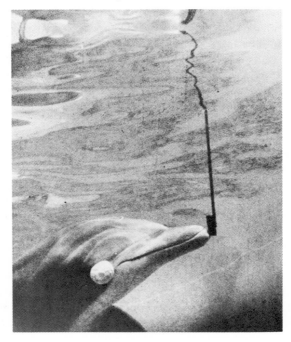

FIG. 46. The eyes of this bottlenose dolphin are covered with rubber blinders for an experiment. After Norris c.s. (1961).

under water and then pick up and make perceptible the waves reflected off solid bodies. The kind of calls emitted by cetaceans is very well suited to such a system. In fact, it has been established that the two principles embodied in submarine-detection devices (tone duration and frequency modulation) are present in the supersonic calls of dolphins. But the data mentioned above prove only that whales can hear and produce supersonic calls; it does not prove that they do in fact use these calls to orient themselves in space. However, American researchers have determined that bottlenose dolphins in the dark or with blinders on their eyes are quite capable of avoiding all sorts of obstacles under water and also of finding and catching fishes (Fig. 46). When they are placed under these conditions, the number of supersonic calls emitted by them increases markedly. So for the present we can rightly assume that whales orient themselves in space through some sort of sonar, even though we would have to eliminate their hearing apparatus or their vocal apparatus to prove this conclusively.

This would explain why even large whales can easily be surrounded with nets—a hunting method that has been a particular favorite in Japan for centuries. The animals are frightened by the nets, which are really an insignificant obstacle for them, and they do not attempt to break through them. If you want to catch dolphins in nets, for example, you must use nets with a large mesh; otherwise they will be perceived by the dolphins and avoided.

The hypothesis of sonar orientation also explains why individual cetaceans or large herds of them occasionally run aground on some beach. Dudok van Heel has pointed out that such beachings almost always occur when the surface of the beach has very little slope to it, or when the bottom is very muddy. In such cases even a sonar apparatus fails. Either there is no echo at all or else it comes from all sides. Under these conditions the whales cannot sound the coast and suddenly find themselves beached.

VIII. *Nutrition and Digestion*

The blue whale is 30 meters long on the average and reaches a maximum length of 38 meters. Its maximum weight amounts to 130,000 kilograms. That is the weight of 4 brontosaurs, 25 elephants, 150 cows, or 1600 human beings (Fig. 47). The fat yield of one such whale is equal to the butterfat yield of 275 cows over the course of a whole year. The blue whale is the largest animal that has ever lived on earth. It was able to attain this enormous size only because it lives constantly in the water. The same holds true for the fin whale (maximum weight, 70 tons), the other baleen whales, and the sperm whale (53 tons).

When an animal grows larger, its volume and hence its weight increases at a cubic rate (x times y times z). But the sustaining strength of its bones and muscles, which must support this weight off the ground, only increases at a square rate (x times y). This is obvious if we consider the strength of a rope. Obviously this power is determined only by the width and thickness of the rope, not by its length. As an animal grows larger, then, the supportive capacity of its bones and muscles vis-à-vis the weight to be carried grows smaller. At some point a weight limit is reached. Beyond that point the animal can no longer stand or move forward on land. In the water, where buoyancy compensates for the animal's weight, there are no limitations in this particular respect.

1 blue whale (30 meters, 130,000 kgs.) weighs as much as:

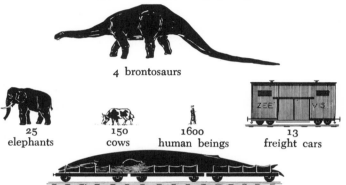

4 brontosaurs

| 25 elephants | 150 cows | 1600 human beings | 13 freight cars |

A whale cannot be transported on an open flat car because a flat car, 10 meters long, has a carrying capacity of only 15,000 kilograms. It would take 9 cars to carry the whale.

FIG. 47. The size and dimensions of a blue whale. After Slijper (1948).

The main food of all baleen whales (except Bryde's whale) consists of small crustaceans. In Antarctic waters the principal food is a crustacean six centimeters long, *Euphausia superba,* generally known as "krill" (Figs. 48 and 49). Clusters of krill may form so thickly in the upper reaches of the Antarctic waters that the sea seems to be a shimmering mass of reddish porridge. The reddish-orange color of the krill results from the presence of carotene, a primary element in the formation of Vitamin A. One can also clearly see the green content of the stomach in these otherwise transparent animalcules. The krill feeds

FIG. 48. When the stomach of a fin whale is cut open, the krill pours out on the deck. Photo by W. L. van Utrecht (Amsterdam).

on diatoms which, like all green plants, are capable of assimilating carbon dioxide and transforming it into organic compounds. The principal reserve material of the diatoms is fat. Once the fat of the microscopic diatom has passed through the krill and then the whale, it becomes whale oil which is used to manufacture margarine or soap.

Obviously enough whales cannot capture the enormous masses of these tiny animalcules with a normal set of

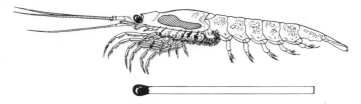

FIG. 49. "Krill," *Euphausia superba Dana.* ⊘ = green; ⊛ = reddish orange. After Mackintosh and Wheeler (1929), altered.

FIG. 50. Head of a fin whale on the quarter deck of the *Willem Barendsz*. The front baleens of the right side are white in color, the back baleens are black. The upper side of the head is turned to the viewer. Photo by W. L. van Utrecht (Amsterdam).

teeth. They need a sieve, such as the kind used to get plankton. The sievelike devices of the whale are the baleens, horny plates hanging down from the gums like a great stage curtain. There are 300 to 400 on each side of the mouth, and they contain hairy fringes on the inner side (Figs. 50–53). When they eat, the whales take a huge amount of water and krill into their mouths, raise the floor of their mouth and the tongue, close their mouth and let the water flow out through the baleen on either side. The krill clings to the hairy fringes and is then transported to the pharynx and the esophagus in some way as yet unknown to us.

The baleens of right whales are long and slender. Greenland right whales have an average length of 3.25 meters and a maximum length of 4.50 meters. Biscayan

FIG. 51. Lower side or bottom of a fin whale's upper jaw showing the inside of the baleens with their hairy fringes. The baleens on the left side have already been stripped away. Photo by W. L. van Utrecht (Amsterdam).

right whales have a maximum length of 2.50 meters. Because of these long baleens the upper jaw of right whales is bent upward and they have a very high lower lip (Fig. 54). The baleens of rorquals have a maximum length of 1 meter (in the blue whale). The upper jaw is flat and there is no raised lower lip. The difference here is apparently connected with the way they take in food. Right whales seem to swim with their mouths open almost all the time, wading, as it were, through the mass of krill in this fashion. By contrast the rorquals seem to take the krill in gulps. These gulps are huge, however, because the grooves in the skin of the lower jaw and the breast enable them to enlarge the size of their mouth enormously. In right whales the krill is constantly being licked off the inner side of the baleens by the tongue, and the tip

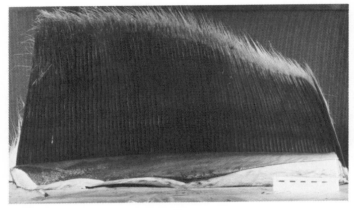

a

b

FIG. 52 a and b. Baleens of a lesser rorqual. a: from the outside; b: from the inside. Photo by W. L. van Utrecht (Amsterdam).

of their tongue is extremely mobile and flexible; it contains many fascicles of muscle. Among rorquals we find a free-wheeling tongue tip only in calves who are still being nursed with their mother's milk. Later on their

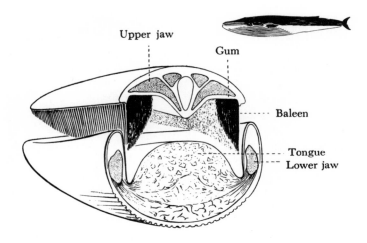

FIG. 53. Schematic drawing of the head of a fin whale with the baleens. After Hentschel (1937), altered.

tongue will be nothing more than an elevation of the floor of their mouth, and it will contain little muscle tissue.

In the sei whale the hairy fringes on the inner side of the baleens are fine and soft, because this whale feeds principally on very small crustaceans and other planktonic organisms. In Bryde's whale, on the other hand, the

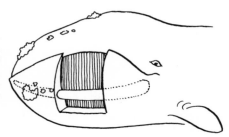

FIG. 54. Schematic drawing of the head of a Biscayan right whale. Part of the lower lip has been cut away showing the position of the baleens. After Matthews (1952).

fringes are hard and thick because their principal food is fish. In the Antarctic the fin whale feeds mainly on krill; in the North Atlantic, however, a considerable portion of its food is fish—chiefly herring.

Naturally all the Odontoceti have teeth in their jaws. The dentures of the individual groups show wide variations, however, in line with their food supply. What Cuvier said over 150 years ago applies here: "Show me your teeth and I will tell you who you are."

The denture of fish-eating dolphins consists of a long row of simple conical teeth with sharp points; in the common porpoise they are leaf-shaped (Fig. 6). The number of teeth ranges from 14 in each half of the jaw in the Irrawaddy dolphin to 68 in each half in the Amazon dolphin (the Boto); the latter is a ferocious predator which feeds on the feared piranha fish. The denture of dolphins only helps them to seize their prey; the latter is not chewed but swallowed whole. For this reason dolphins must restrict their food to fish which are not too large. We know of one case where a bottlenose dolphin choked on a 1.20-meter-long shark.

This restriction does not apply to the killer whale (*Orcinus orca*), a dolphin which can be up to 9.50 meters in length. Because of its extreme voraciousness it has earned the nickname "killer" or "murderer." It is doubtful that any human being has ever been killed by a killer whale, yet every sailor grows uncomfortable when its razor-sharp dorsal fin appears above the surface of the sea. The fact is that the killer whale is not a fish eater. It prefers to eat birds and aquatic mammals. Its chief foods are penguins, common porpoises, dolphins, narwhals, belugas, seals, and sea lions. It will not take on grown walruses, but the large baleen whales are often attacked by herds of three to forty killer whales. The herd of predators will tear off pieces of flesh from the flippers and lips and tongue of the large but clumsy baleen whales, causing them to bleed profusely. When they lose so much blood that they cannot survive, the killer whales will move in to eat them in earnest. The slow-swimming gray whales often suffer a great deal at the hands of the killers, and the latter are a serious threat to the young calves of all the great whales. In each half of their jaw the killer whales have ten to fourteen sharp teeth; these may be worn down in older members of the species. When their prey is not too large, they will gulp it down whole. In the crop of a 7.5-meter-long killer Eschricht found no less than 13 fully intact porpoises and 14 seals; a fifteenth seal was found in the pharynx (Fig. 55).

Among many groups of sea inhabitants there are species which specialize in eating cuttlefish (Fig. 56). Since cuttlefish generally do not move very fast and since they are extremely tender and soft, one notes a reduction of teeth in all cuttlefish eaters. Consider the lower Miocene beaked whale from Patagonia, *Diochoticus*. Its long jaw still has 23 well-developed teeth in the upper jaw and 19 in the lower jaw. This animal lived about 18 million years ago. Now consider the upper Miocene whale from Belgium, *Mioziphius*. Its upper jaw still contains 40 teeth, but its lower denture has been reduced to 2 teeth. In another species from the upper Miocene, *Choneziphius*, there is scarcely any trace of teeth sockets in the upper jaw. The recent species, *Tasmacetus shepherdi*, was only discovered about twenty years ago in New Zealand; it still has 19 well-developed teeth in its upper jaw and 27 in its lower jaw. Among the other recent representatives of the Ziphiidae (e.g., the bottlenose whale), we find only 1 or 2 teeth in each half of its jaw (Fig. 57). But with X-rays or careful dissection one can establish that there is usually a whole set of rudimentary teeth in the gums.

The pilot whale and the false killer whale are also cuttlefish eaters, even though on occasion their food may consist wholly or partially of fish. In each half of the jaw

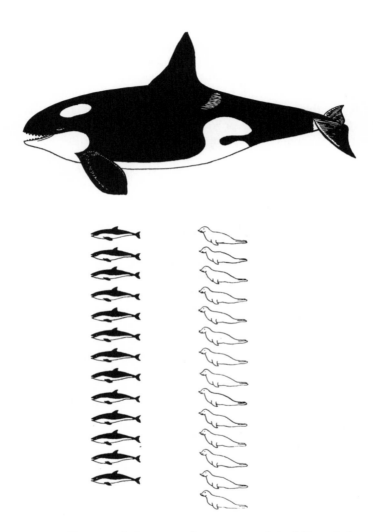

FIG. 55. Content of the crop of a 7.5-meter-long killer whale (*Orcinus orca*).

FIG. 56. The stomach content of a sperm whale consists chiefly of cuttlefish. Photo by W. L. van Utrecht (Amsterdam).

they have only 8 to 11 teeth. The denture of Risso's whale is reduced even further. The six pair of teeth in its lower jaw are poorly developed, and no teeth are present in its upper jaw.

The denture of the sperm whale is also reduced. All it has is 18 to 30 pair of teeth in its lower jaw (Fig. 58). These teeth no longer have their own individual sockets; rather, they are set in a common bony furrow. The connective tissue of the lower jaw is so solid and tough that many a souvenir hunter has lost his knife blade trying to cut out the teeth of a stranded or captured sperm whale. When the sperm whale closes its very small lower jaw, the teeth fit into corresponding holes in the upper jaw. The latter is without teeth, apart from the rudimentary

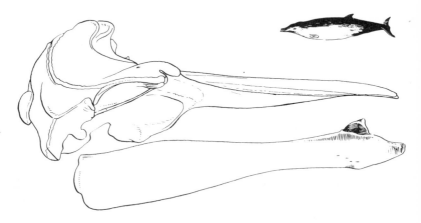

FIG. 57. Skull of a beaked whale with just a single tooth in its lower jaw. After Van Beneden and Gervais (1880).

teeth that were noted as far back as 1771. These tooth rudiments are usually buried in the gum, but now and then they may also show up on the outer surface. In 1937 an 18-meter-long male sperm whale was beached at Bresken; on each side of his upper jaw Boschma found 15 rudimentary teeth of this sort.

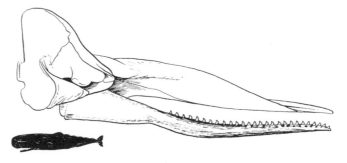

FIG. 58. Skull of a sperm whale. After Van Beneden and Gervais (1880).

The teeth of the lower jaw can be about 20 centimeters long. They are composed of very fine ivory, but they do not seem to play such an important role in feeding as one would expect. When the newborn calf of the sperm whale is dropped, its teeth have not yet broken through. They come through only at puberty. Thus for at least three years the young sperm whale captures its food without the use of teeth. The food of the adult sperm whales is usually cuttlefish ranging in length from 90 to 120 centimeters (Fig. 56). But they can also handle the largest species of all, *Architeuthis*. At a shore station in the Azores, Clarke found a specimen of this giant cuttlefish in the stomach of a sperm whale. The specimen was 10.5 meters long (with tentacles) and weighed 184 kilograms. That is equivalent to the weight of two adult human beings and a child.

If the story of Jonah occurred exactly as we are told, then it must have been a sperm whale that swallowed Jonah and then spit him up again; for the diameter of the pharynx and the esophagus in the large baleen whales is much too small. It does seem that on one occasion a sailor was attacked and swallowed by a sperm whale, but no scientist now believes that a human being could survive a stay in the stomach of such an animal. A human being would suffocate, although not from lack of room, since the stomach of a large baleen whale has a capacity of approximately 1000 liters.

If we correlate this figure and the stomach capacity of other cetaceans with their bodily size, we cannot say that the capacity of the cetacean stomach is large. A large stomach capacity is not to be expected in a carnivore, and we would not stress the point here if it were not for the fact that the general structure of the cetacean stomach is akin to that of the herbivore. It consists, first, of a large crop covered with a glittering white, cutaneous, mucous membrane. No glands discharge into this crop

(Fig. 59). The main stomach, whose mucous membrane is violet-colored and velvetlike, is next. Here we find the characteristic gastric glands secreting pepsin and hydrochloric acid. Small amounts of lipase are also found in this section. The normal pyloric glands discharge into the third section of the stomach.

Even though the divisions of the cetacean stomach are strongly reminiscent of those to be found in herbivorous ungulates or the leaf-eating Guereza monkeys, the function of the cetacean crop must be entirely different because no cellulose-splitting bacteria or one-celled organisms are to be found there. In all probability the cetacean crop has the same function as the avian gizzard; in the latter food is pulverized by strong muscular contractions with the help of sand and pebbles. We can easily picture a similar function for the cetacean crop since whales do not chew their food. Now and then sand and gravel have been found in the crop of toothed whales, but this material is not indispensable because the armor

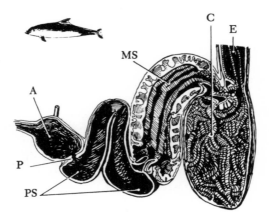

FIG. 59. Stomach of the bottlenose dolphin. E: esophagus; C: crop; MS: main stomach; PS: pyloric stomach; P: pylorus; A: ampulla of the duodenum. After Pernkopf (1937).

covering of the krill and the bones of the fish provide fine material for crushing the food. The validity of our explanation is corroborated by the fact that the crop is entirely absent in beaked whales, which eat soft cuttle-fish. But it is present in sperm whales, whose food is far less specialized.

In the rest of the intestinal canal, a small caecum is present only in baleen whales and in the Ganges dolphin, and that there is no sharp distinction between the small intestine and the large intestine. The latter fact is true of most carnivores. When one considers the size of the ceta-ceans and then compares the length of their intestine with that of other mammals, one finds a very close corre-

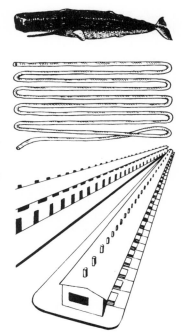

FIG. 60. A 17-meter-long sperm whale has an intestine that is 160 meters long. That is equiv-alent to a street with 25 houses of the above type on either side.

spondence with other fish eaters, e.g., with the Pteropoda. Relatively speaking, only the sperm whale has a very long intestine. In the living specimen its absolute length is about 160 meters (Fig. 60).

We do not know why the sperm whale has such a long intestine. But we cannot conclude this discussion of the whale's digestive system, and particularly of the sperm whale's intestine, without mentioning ambergris. This magical product evokes visions of enormous riches garnered by poor people on some lonely beach or from the surface of the sea. It was first used by the Arabs. Both among them and in medieval Europe it was regarded as a desirable aphrodisiac, and it was used in love potions. Later it became an indispensable ingredient in the perfume industry, which still retains a certain interest in it today. How ambergris comes to be is still not known fully, but we do know that it is a concretion which arises in the intestinal canal of some sperm whales under abnormal conditions. The concretions can be very large, and pieces weighing 400 to 500 kilograms have been found. The raw material for the formation of ambergris comes from the contents of the intestine; in the laboratory people have managed to manufacture an ambergrislike substance from the excrement of the sperm whale.

IX. *Metabolism and Water Conservation*

Whales are voracious animals. Dudok van Heel had to feed 10 to 12 kilograms of mackerel a day to his porpoises in order to keep them properly nourished. That is quite a hefty ration when one realizes that a large common porpoise has about the same body weight as an adult human being. Naturally enough there are no precise data on the great whales, but we can reasonably assume that a few tons of krill per day is not too low an estimate. When we also advert to the fact that the food in question is usually a fatty one rich in calories, then it becomes clear that whales possess a very high metabolism. One estimate for the bottlenose dolphins in the New York Aquarium was that each animal required 108 calories per kilogram of weight per day. By contrast a human being, whose size does not differ markedly from the size of a bottlenose dolphin, needs only 53 calories per kilogram.

The reasons for this high metabolism in the cetacean body are not hard to find. First and foremost is the fact that these animals are almost always in motion. They cannot retire to an easy chair or to a quiet lair; indeed they must make swimming motions even while they sleep. Secondly, there is the fact that the heat loss of these animals is much greater than the heat loss in land animals because thermal conductivity in water is about 27 times as great as that in air. Moreover, the steady flow of water along the whale's body causes rapid heat dissipation.

When we realize that a human being in 0°C water loses consciousness in about ten minutes, we can appreciate the problems faced by whales in conserving heat.

At this point the reader might be inclined to jump in with an explanation: the problem is solved by the heat-insulating layer of blubber. It is true that whales, like human beings and other mammals, possess a skin covering composed of three layers: the epidermis, the true skin, and a subcutaneous connective tissue. Their epidermis is very thin. In the great whales it is just about 5 to 7 millimeters thick, and the outer horny layers are scarcely one millimeter thick. The fat-free corium is also very thin, usually being only a few millimeters thick. For this reason it cannot even be used to make leather. The skins of the narwhal, the beluga whale, and certain river dolphins are exceptions to this rule. In addition, the skin of the penis of the great whales can also be tanned and converted into leatherware. Many whalers have used this material to get themselves a leather jacket or a soft cushion for their favorite easy chair. In whales as in hogs the layer of blubber is located in the subcutaneous connective tissue. This is a thick layer of connective tissue with large conglomerations of fat cells and relatively slight blood supply.

In right whales the layer of blubber is very thick. It averages about 50 centimeters in thickness, but it can reach 70 centimeters. In sperm whales and humpback whales its average thickness is 12 to 18 centimeters; in blue whales and fin whales it averages 8 to 14 centimeters; the sei whale has the thinnest layer of blubber, averaging 5 to 8 centimeters. However, these figures are only averages. The thickness of the layer of blubber is very different in different regions of the body and among whales of different lengths. What is more, pregnant females have a very thick layer of blubber whereas lactating females have a very thin layer of blubber. Needless to say, the thickness of the blubber layer depends greatly on the season of the year. Among those species which migrate regularly (see chapter 10), the blubber layer is thin when they arrive in polar waters and it is at its thickest when they leave these waters again.

It is noteworthy that in the case of the Antarctic rorquals, at least, the layer of blubber scarcely increases at all after the end of January. Other reserves of fat stored in its body are stored in the bones, or in the muscles, or in the body cavity, between different organs. It seems that if the layer of blubber were to grow thicker than 14 centimeters (approximately), then the whale would no longer be able to loose the heat produced by its forward motion. It would then be forced to swim very, very slowly or else it would perish from heat prostration amid the polar ice. The fact is that these animals do not have sweat glands—the sweat would not evaporate in water anyway—and the arrangement of their skin vessels is designed more to retain heat than to dissipate it.

One fortunate circumstance for the regulation of body temperature is the fact that temperature fluctuations from day to day are slight in water. The average body temperature of all cetaceans is probably around 35.5°C. For mammals in general that is an extremely low figure; most mammals have a body temperature that is noticeably above that of man.

Knowing that cetaceans have a high metabolism, we are not surprised to find that their endocrine glands are well developed compared to those of land mammals. To be specific, the weight of the thyroid gland and the weight of the suprarenal capsule exceed those of the corresponding organs in land mammals. Only the Japanese use the products of these organs and the insulin from the pancreas for pharmaceutical purposes. But on Norwegian ships the anterior lobe of the pituitary gland is taken to make ACTH.[1]

A detailed treatment of the other organs regulating metabolism would exceed the proper confines of this book. But we must say something about the kidneys because those of animals living in salt water must make certain characteristic adaptations to their environment. Basically vertebrates are not made for living in sea water. The salt concentration in their blood and their body fluids is lower than that in sea water. Among invertebrates, by contrast, there is usually a balance between the salt concentration inside and outside their bodies. Among vertebrates the mucous membranes of the mouth, pharynx, and intestine usually work as semi-permeable membranes to restore equilibrium; they let water through but not salt. For this reason, and because there is a general tendency to restore equilibrium on either side of these membranes, water is continually being withdrawn from the body of vertebrates which live in the sea. The animals compensate for this loss by drinking water or taking in water with their food. In this way a large quantity of salt is taken in once again. In bony fishes this salt is separated from the body by chloride-secreting cells in their gills.

Mammals do not have such cells. What is more, the cetaceans do not have sweat glands. Hence the excess salt can only be removed through their kidneys. Fetcher has shown that now and then bottlenose dolphins can secrete urine with a high salt content in a relatively short period of time, but that their urine generally shows the normal salt concentration for mammals. This means that the excess salt in the body can only be removed by the production of a great deal of urine, which in turn means

---

1. ACTH, the adrenocorticotropic hormone, stimulates the adrenal cortex.

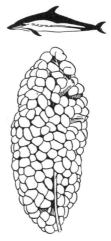

FIG. 61. Kidney of the common dolphin.
After Anthony (1922).

that considerable quantities of water are required for this
purpose. Apparently water is available to the cetaceans
on the one hand because they can neither evaporate it or
sweat it out, while on the other hand much water is released through their high metabolism (i.e., in the burning
of fat).

Unfortunately we do not yet know for sure whether
whales do in fact produce that great a quantity of urine
per day. But this is very likely because their kidneys are
very large in comparison with those of land mammals.
The weight of a cetacean kidney is about double that of
a land mammal of equal size. What is more, water secre-
tion takes place primarily in the cortical substance of
the kidney and, in cetaceans, this cortical substance is
greatly enlarged because the kidney is divided up into
numerous tiny lobes. Each of these lobes really consti-
tutes a little kidney in itself (Fig. 61). A similar system
of *reniculi* is found in certain land mammals such as cows
and bears, but the number of *reniculi* is much greater in
cetaceans: 250 in each kidney of the common porpoise,

450 in each kidney of dolphins, and about 3000 in each kidney of the large whales. In the Ganges dolphin, which lives in fresh water, Anderson found only 80 *reniculi* per kidney, and the kidneys themselves were much smaller than those of salt-water dwellers in relationship to body size.

x. *Geographical Distribution and Migrations*

As we saw in earlier chapters, the great whales generally feed solely on small planktonic crustaceans called "krill," and the latter depend for their food on small plant organisms known as diatoms. The existence of diatoms, in turn, depends on the presence of carbon dioxide, oxygen, and inorganic nutrients in sea water.

Carbon dioxide and oxygen are present in larger quantities in cold water than they are in warm water. Moreover, bacteria do not thrive as well in cold waters as they do in tropical and subtropical waters, and they often consume the existing food supply. As a general rule, then, we find little plankton in warm waters and much plankton in cold waters. The inorganic salts are brought to the southern hemisphere by a water current from the tropics. It flows deep below the surface and then rises to the top at around 53°S latitude. This addition of large quantities of inorganic food particles to a body of water rich in oxygen and carbon dioxide creates an ideal environment for the development of plant and animal plankton.

In general plankton is distributed quite evenly over the whole area between 50°S and the Antarctic continent. But the whale's food, krill, is an exception to this rule. It apparently flourishes best in very cold water. Three English biologists (Fraser, Bargmann, and Marr) have shown that large concentrations of krill show up in only two areas: in the zone of the easterly wind drift between about 63°S and the Antarctic continent and in the Weddell current, which flows northeastward from the Weddell Sea to about 50°S (Fig. 62).

The main contingent of Antarctic whales are to be found in these two zones, but only in summer. When the temperature drops in autumn, the pack ice shifts slowly northward. In September its northern boundary limit is around 55°S latitude. Now the whole area in which krill is present is covered with pack ice and inaccessible to the whales. They can surface and breathe in drift ice, but they cannot do these things in an area of solid pack ice. So the great whales migrate northward in March and April. It seems that a certain number of them do spend the winter in the open waters along the northern rim of the pack ice, but the main contingent of whales migrates to tropical and subtropical waters. This has been verified by the catch figures from shore stations in Africa, Australia, and South America.

Much less is known about the behavior and distribution of whales in warm waters than about their behavior and distribution in the polar zones. But in 1951 the National Institute of Oceanography (Wormley, near London) began a program of trying to get merchant marine officers interested in taking sightings of whales on their cruises. With the help of these men the Dutch Committee for Whale Research (T.N.O.) collected 4000 observations between 1954 and 1958; they dealt with approximately 11,000 whales and covered seas all over the world. Study of these data revealed that the whales apparently concentrated in certain areas of the tropics, most likely because those particular waters had a very rich supply of food. Fishery statistics indicate that the largest catches of tropical fish occur in the same areas where large concentrations of dolphins have been seen. The areas in question are the Arabian Sea, the Gulf of Aden, the Caribbean Sea, and certain areas around Dakar and New-

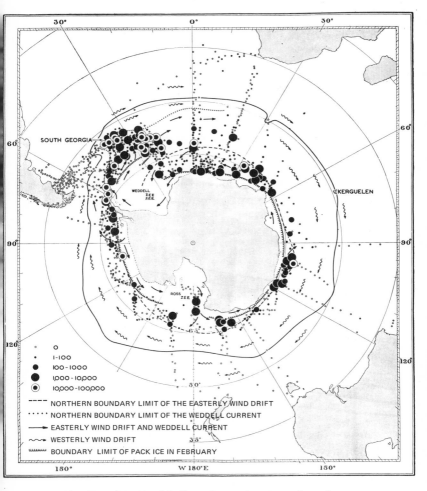

FIG. 62. Distribution of krill in Antarctic waters from January to March. The size of the dots represents the number of animalcules taken up by a plankton net 1 meter in diameter when it was drawn across the surface of the water. After Marr (1956).

foundland. In fact it is quite likely that each year a portion of the Arctic and Antarctic whale stock does not migrate to polar waters but rather spends the summer in tropical or subtropical waters. And the makeup and size of this group probably varies from year to year. As yet we cannot even make a rough estimate of the number of whales which spend the summer in the tropics or spend the winter along the northern fringes of the ice packs. But our impression is that the majority of whales do indeed make the 17,000 kilometer journey from the polar ice to the tropics and back again each year. While the whales may find some food in the tropics, they are still quite thin when they return to colder waters.

The oldest data on whale migrations comes from the latter half of the nineteenth century. Norwegian shore stations brought in blue whales bearing American explosive harpoons in their bodies. Apparently they had been hunted off the American coast. Systematic marking, such as that which is done in avian research, first became possible in 1931 when the "Discovery Committee" succeeded in developing a satisfactory whale marker. It is a rust-free metal dart with a lead tip and is about 27 centimeters long. It can be shot off by an ordinary cartridge from a gun that is usually mounted on a ship's grenade harpoon (Fig. 63). The inscription on the metal capsule promises a reward to the finder, and the marker itself apparently feels like nothing more than a pin-prick to a whale.

From 1934 to 1939 the *William Scoresby* shot off 5063 markers. As of today about 400 have been recovered. The markers are usually found in the whale's back muscles.

REWARD PAID FOR RETURN TO DISCOVERY COMMITTEE COLONIAL OFFICE LONDON

FIG. 63. Whale marker of the National Institute of Oceanography (Wormley, near London).

Often they may be buried so well that they are not noticed on the factory ship during the flensing process and
only show up in the cooker. When this happens, it is no
longer possible to say with certainty from which whale
the markers came. The marking process is harmless and
the marker itself can be carried for years by a whale, as
is evident from the fact that each year we are recovering
markers from the 1930s. Since whale marking is a very
costly procedure, we have not been able to continue with
this procedure in the same way since World War II.
Today whales are usually marked by certain catcher
boats at the beginning of the whaling season. But of
course many of these whales are shot in the very same
season.

International whaling statistics have shown that whales
are not evenly distributed over the waters of Antarctica.
They are concentrated in six specific regions, probably
because krill is particularly abundant there. These six
regions are located: (1) south of the Atlantic Ocean (20°–
70° W); (2) south of Africa (20°–40°E); (3) southwest
of Australia (80°–110°E); (4) southeast of Australia
(150°–170°E); (5) southeast of New Zealand (160°–
140°W); (6) southwest of South America (110°–70°W).

In the case of the humpback whale, the data derived
from the marking process has shown that the separation
between the individual stocks in the Antarctic region is
also caused by the fact that their migration routes are
pretty much restricted to the coastal waters off the con-
tinents. For the most part they travel north and south
along the meridians; hence they only populate the aforementioned regions of Antarctica (Fig. 64). There is practically no interchange between the individual stocks in
the Antarctic Ocean. But a humpback whale from the
stock in the southern Atlantic Ocean may migrate to the
west coast of Africa and then join a herd that belongs to
an area south of Africa.

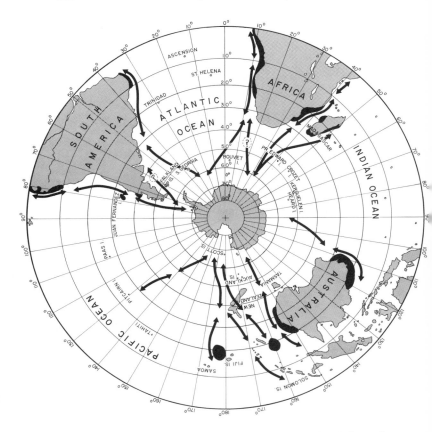

FIG. 64. Distribution and migrations of the humpback whale in the southern hemisphere.

In the case of the blue whale and the fin whale, the stocks are less sharply divided. Whale marking has shown that they do indeed migrate mainly from south to north and back again, but that there is a higher degree of interchange than in the case of the humpback whale (Fig. 65). In the case of fin whales this interchange does not

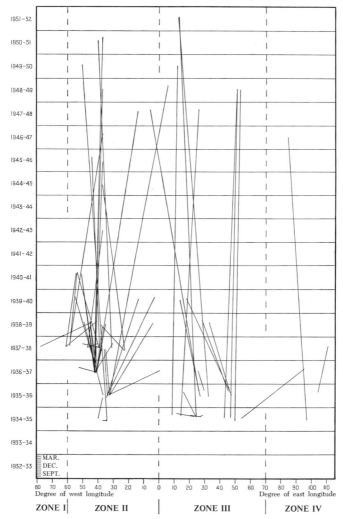

FIG. 65. Time chart showing dispersal in fin whales of unknown sex. Each line connects the location in Antarctic waters where the whale was marked, to the vicinity where the marking was recovered. After Brown (1954).

exceed a distance of 50°, in the case of blue whales it does not exceed a distance of 87°. The interchange itself can take place in tropical waters or in the Antarctic itself. We know one case of a blue whale which travelled a distance of 1900 miles in 47 days in the Antarctic Ocean.

The migration routes of blue whales and fin whales also lie farther off the coast than those of humpback whales. While a certain number of fin whales (usually youngsters) are caught by shore stations in South America and South Africa, blue whales seem to migrate so far from land that they are practically never caught by tropical whalers. The same holds true for most adult fin whales. The behavior of these two species does differ in another respect. The blue whale resides mainly in the zone of drift ice. By contrast most fin whales are found outside this zone in open waters. As yet we have no explanation for this difference.

In general terms the migrations of whales in the Arctic Ocean accord with those of their Antarctic relatives. They too migrate to tropical waters in the winter. Because the southern stocks are then in the Antarctic region for the most part, our impression is that intermingling of the two stocks is an exceptional occurrence. It does take place now and then, however, as Zenkovitch has shown. He pointed out the fact that around Kamatchatka blue whales and fin whales have been caught which were infected with southern skin parasites (*Penella*). Migration seems to be less marked among fin whales in the Atlantic Ocean than among their relatives in the waters of the Pacific. A considerable portion of the North Atlantic stock stays in the temperate zone both in summer and in winter. This seems to be related to the fact that the fin whales of the North Atlantic eat a lot of fish, particularly herring.

In broad outlines the distribution and migrations of the gray whale, the lesser rorqual, the bottlenose whale, and the Biscayan right whale agree with those of the blue whale and the fin whale. By contrast the Greenland right whale, the pigmy right whale, the beluga whale, and the narwhal generally do not leave the polar waters and make only limited journeys within this area. The sei whale and Bryde's whale live in tropical and subtropical waters for the most part. Only a small portion of sei whales venture to feed on Arctic or Antarctic krill for a short period during the summer.

Female and juvenile sperm whales can be found only in the waters between 40°N and 40°S. We know of only two strandings outside this zone where females were included in the herd. One occurred in December 1723 at Hamburg (54°N). The other occurred in March 1784 at Audierne (Brittany; 48°N). All other strandings on the English, Belgian, Dutch, and German coast involved adult or practically adult males which were not able to win a harem (see chapter 6) and which generally migrate to the icy north or south in summer. These animals are distributed all over the tropics. But certain migrations and the existence of certain large concentrations is closely tied up with the presence of their food supply (cuttlefish). They are found in great numbers around the Azores, the Galapagos Islands, and the west coast of southern Africa.

XI. *Reproduction*

The main concern of applied whaling research is to ascertain how many whales may be caught each year without detriment to the whale stocks. Naturally this presumes exact data on the yearly population increase in whales: that is to say, a precise knowledge and understanding of their reproduction. For this reason applied research workers have delved deeply into the matter of cetacean reproduction in recent decades, and they have come up with a body of factual material that was not at our disposal before.

We are still not as informed as we would like to be about certain processes in the reproductive cycle. Insofar as the great whales are concerned, for example, we still have little data about the mating process. We do know that their mating almost always takes place in warm waters, and we also know that the mating act itself takes place very quickly. Everyone who has observed copulation among the large whales and among dolphins, both in aquariums and on the open sea, talks about a process lasting from five to twenty seconds. This coincides with the behavior of most artiodactyls (cows, sheep, deer). The split-second mating in turn is intimately bound up with the structure of the male sex organ.

As is the case with the aforementioned artiodactyls, the cetacean penis consists of a solid strand of elastic tissue that is from 2.5 to 3 meters long in the great whales. This strand of tissue lies in a sling below the peritoneum, and

117

it is extruded only when the whale is sexually aroused. The extrusion is due primarily to the elasticity of the sex organ and only slightly to a flow of blood into it; for this reason it can take place very quickly.

The position of the two partners vis-à-vis each other can be quite varied. Dolphins have been observed swimming alongside each other while the male bent his tail under the female's body. Among the large whales, mating seems to take place almost always in a stomach-to-stomach position (Fig. 66). The animals may swim along the surface of the water in a lateral position, or they may rise vertically out of the water with their stomachs facing

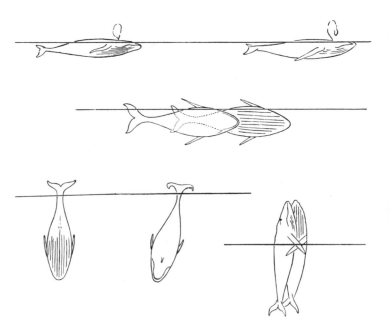

FIG. 66. Sketch of the mating of two humpback whales. After Nishiwaki and Hayashi (1951).

each other. The latter position has been observed among humpback whales, fin whales, and sperm whales. All observers agree that the mating act itself is preceded by prolonged and tender foreplay. The pair make swimming motions in each other's direction and stroke each other with their bodies and flippers. Observations of pilot whales on the open sea indicate that they can rise vertically out of the water as far as their flukes (Fig. 67). At the same time they may playfully bite each other's jaws and flukes as frisky puppies do.

The male sex organ has the same general structure it has in other mammals. The testicles do not lie in a scrotum outside the body but at the rear of the abdominal cavity behind the kidneys, as is the case with elephants and armadillos. In a blue whale each of the organs can attain a length of 80 centimeters and a weight of 45 kilograms. The female sex organs consist of a vagina with a heavily folded mucous membrane, a two-horned uterus, the Fallopian tubes, and the ovaries, which are located at

FIG. 67. A pilot whale in the vertical position during love play. They may also surface in this position outside the mating season. Photo by Th. Carels ('s-Gravenhage).

the exact same place in the abdominal cavity as the male testicles are. In large whales these organs weigh 5 to 10 kilograms. But the factory ship *Balaena* once took aboard a pregnant blue whale, 83 feet long, with an ovary weighing 30 kilograms.

The ovaries of toothed whales look exactly like the ovaries of other mammals. In the baleen whales, by contrast, they look like a cluster of grapes. For even when the female baleen whale is not in heat, there are a whole cluster of half-ripe follicles bulging out on the surface of the organ like so many grapes (Fig. 68). Normally only one of these follicles develops to full maturity in a given period of heat. With ovulation the follicle bursts and the egg is ejected through the Fallopian tube into the uterus. The follicle has a diameter of three to six centimeters, but the egg itself is only about 0.1 to 0.2 millimeters in size as is the case with most other mammals.

Just as is true of other mammals, a *corpus luteum* (Fig. 68) develops from the empty follicle shell after ovulation. In toothed whales it has the typical yellow color; in baleen whales it is pink. The *corpus luteum* produces a hormone which abets the attachment of the embryo to the wall of the uterus. If the egg is not fertilized, then no attachment takes place and the *corpus luteum* soon shrivels up into a white mass of connective tissue (*corpus albicans*). If attachment does take place and the embryo undergoes further development, then the *corpus luteum* grows markedly. It develops into a ball attached to the ovary, having a diameter of 11 to 20 centimeters (in fin whales and blue whales) and a weight of 0.8 to 7.5 kilograms. It remains present in this form throughout the pregnancy, degenerating into a *corpus albicans* only after the birth.

In large whales the *corpora albicantia* initially have a diameter of 8 to 14 centimeters; later they diminish to only one or two centimeters. Unlike the case of other mammals, the *corpora albicantia* of whales and dolphins

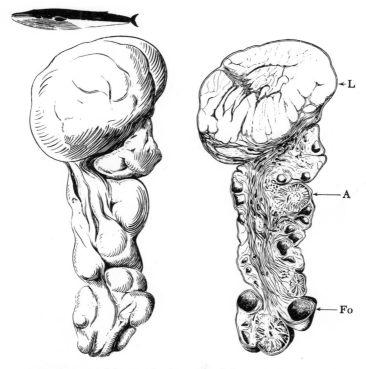

FIG. 68. Ovary and longitudinal section of this organ in a pregnant fin whale. L: *corpus luteum;* A: *corpus albicans;* Fo: follicle.

are not reabsorbed by the surrounding tissue. They remain in the ovary as vestiges of each ovulation throughout the life of the animal (Fig. 68). This is a stroke of luck for biologists because it enables them to determine how many times an adult female has ovulated during her life. But only the number of ovulations can be determined because a *corpus albicans* formed after a pregnancy has the same look and structure as one formed after an ovulation that did not result in pregnancy.

Whales and dolphins do not enjoy the luxury of tucking their young away in a nest or burrow. As soon as the calves leave the protection of their mother's body, they are in the same position as colts and cow calves. They still get their nourishment from their mother, but they no longer derive warmth from her and they must swim along with her right from the start. This means that the whale calf is big and very well-developed at birth—like a colt but unlike kittens and puppies.

We would not expect a tiny suckling from a mother who is 30 meters long and weighs 100 tons. But we can still be surprised to find that a newborn blue whale is 7 meters long and weighs about 2000 kilograms (Fig. 69). The newborn fin whale is 6.5 meters long and weighs

FIG. 69. 7-meter-long fetus of a blue whale, almost completely delivered. Note the umbilical cord with the distinctive amniotic pearls. Photo by W. L. van Utrecht (Amsterdam).

about 1800 kilograms, and the newborn sperm whale is 4 meters long and weighs about 1300 kilograms. Newborn dolphins are even bigger in comparison with their mothers. They can have 45 percent of her length and 15 percent of her weight. All this means that these animals generally bear only one calf in each pregnancy. Twins show up in 1 percent of the cases, as is true in the case of human beings and horses. Triplets can also be born. Indeed six embryos have been observed in a cetacean uterus, but we have no way of knowing whether the birth of sextuplets is actually possible.

The size and full development of the newborn calf also means that the gestation period, at least in the case of common porpoises and common dolphins, is relatively long. As is the case with much larger horse and cow, it lasts 10 to 12 months. What is surprising is the fact that the large baleen whales gestate only about eleven months (Fig. 76), whereas the gestation periods of the much smaller rhinoceros and elephant are 19 months and 22 months respectively. The eggs of all these animals are about the same size. This means that the embryos of the large whales grow much more quickly and that their food demands on their mother's bodies are much greater than those made by dolphin embryos. Only the sperm whale is an exception to this rule. The female of this species gestates 16 months. Japanese researchers have claimed that this same gestation period holds true for the killer whale of the North Pacific.

In toothed whales the embryo is almost always located in the left horn of the uterus, even when the right ovary has undergone ovulation (Fig. 70). The right horn contains only a part of the placenta. In all cetaceans the latter is a diffuse, epithelio-chorial placenta, as is the case with horses and pigs. In baleen whales about 50 percent of the embryo is located in the right horn; the rest of the embryo is located in the left horn.

FIG. 70. Pregnant uterus of a common porpoise. The embryo is in the left horn. The right horn holds one of the fetal envelopes (the Allantois) which forms a part of the placenta. After Wislocki (1933).

The birth process of the great whales has never been observed. The sparse data we do possess about this event comes exclusively from females that were stranded or captured during birth. Live-action observation of the birth process has occurred only in the case of porpoises and dolphins (the common dolphin, the bottlenose dolphin, the spotted dolphin) living in captivity. In the case of the bottlenose dolphin in particular, close observation of the birth process has been feasible in many instances at American aquariums. At the start of labor the female begins to swim more slowly. The other female members of the herd stay close to her all the time, apparently to protect her and make sure that she is not separated from the herd. Labor lasts from one-half to a full hour and then, with a number of violent contractions, the tail of the youngster protrudes from the genital orifice (Figs. 71 and 72).

This point is noteworthy. Any expert will tell you that head-first birth is the rule among those land mammals which bear one single large youngster (horses, cows, hu-

FIG. 71. Birth of a bottlenose dolphin at the Florida Marineland Aquarium. Photo by J. R. Eastman (Miami).

man beings), and that a breach birth always entails great danger for the life of the fetus. The danger with a breach birth is that the umbilical cord may rip too early or be snipped off in the mother's pelvis, or that premature breathing efforts by the fetus may arise for one reason or another. If the youngster breathes while its snout is still inside its mother's body, then it may take nonsterile blood, mucous, or amniotic fluid into its lungs. This can lead to infection or suffocation.

Apparently whales are not subject to this danger, first of all because the umbilical cord is so long (Fig. 73) that it is stretched taut only when the head of the youngster leaves its mother's body. The umbilical cord is not bitten off; it rips at a weak spot on the abdomen of the fetus, as is the case with horses and cows. Secondly, there is no

FIG. 72. A common porpoise which got caught in a shrimp net and suffocated during the birth of its young. The flukes of the fetus have already appeared. Photo by W. L. van Utrecht (Amsterdam).

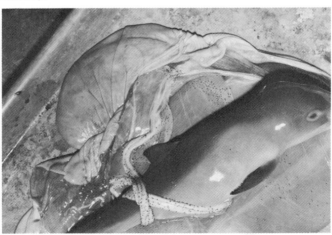

FIG. 73. Male fetus of a common porpoise. Part of the fetal envelopes have been cut away but the allantois is still intact. Note the length of the umbilical cord (with amniotic pearls) looped around the fetus. Photo by W. L. van Utrecht (Amsterdam).

danger because the animals are always born under water and the first breath occurs only when the newborn whale's blowhole is exposed to air above the surface of the water.

Thus we know now why a breach birth does not represent a danger for whales. But we do not yet know why this position occurs in contrast to that typical among all land mammals. The head-first birth common among land mammals is based on the positional adaptation of the fetus to the distribution of space in the mother's abdominal cavity and on the distribution of the fetal mass. Thus in quadrupeds the large and heavy hindquarters are always situated forward and down in the abdominal cavity, while the extremely small and flexible head is located back and up in the vicinity of the female genital orifice. In whales, however, the head is very big while the tail is thin and flexible. Thus it is the latter which is situated near the genital orifice, thereby conforming to the spatial relationships and to the constrictions of the uterus (Fig. 74).

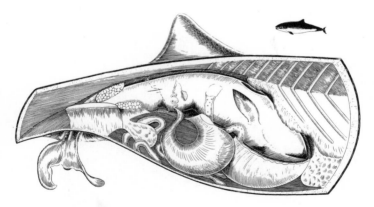

FIG. 74. Schematic diagram of the abdominal cavity of the porpoise depicted in Figure 72. The abdominal cavity has been opened on the right to show the position of the fetus. After Slijper (1956).

As soon as the youngster is born, its mother pushes it to the surface of the water. In this activity and in her further care of the young, the mother is frequently helped by another adult member of the herd nicknamed an "aunt." Such "aunties" have been observed elsewhere only among hippopotamuses and elephants. The afterbirth, which appears between 1½ to 10 hours later, is not eaten. The mother pays it no further notice.

Among blue whales and fin whales the calves are suckled up to the age of 5 to 7 months (Fig. 76). Among most other cetaceans suckling continues for almost a full year, but common porpoises and humpback whales are weaned after 8 months and 10 months respectively. The suckling takes place under water (Fig. 75), as is the case with sea cows and hippopotamuses. The nipples are located in skin grooves on both sides of the female genital orifice. Due to the pressure prevailing in the mammary glands, they come forth during suckling. But because

FIG. 75. Suckling bottlenose dolphin at the Florida Marineland Aquarium. Photo by F. S. Essapian (Miami).

the young animals do not possess real lips, they can only embrace the nipples with their tongue and press against them with their gums. The milk is then sprayed over the upper ridge of the tongue into their gullet.

Rhinoceruses wean their young only after 14 months, and wild cattle often continue nursing for two years. The nursing period of the large whales is surprisingly short by comparison, especially when we realize that a young blue whale grows about 9 meters in seven months, i.e., about 4½ centimeters per day. During this period its weight increases from 2 to 23 tons, i.e., about 100 kilograms per day. This enormous increase in weight is possible only because the milk is very highly concentrated. The water content of the milk is 40 to 50 percent, as opposed to 80 to 90 percent among land mammals, and the milk is also extraordinarily rich. Its fat content is 40 to 50 percent (2 to 17 percent in land mammals), and its protein content is double that of the milk found in land mammals. Calcium and phosphorus are also abundant, to provide for the whale's skeletal growth. Only the sugar content (1 to 2 percent) is lower than that in land mammals (3 to 8 percent).

In order to have a good idea of the procreation rate among whales, we must have other data besides those given above. We must know at what age the animals reach puberty and become sexually mature. We must know to what age they remain capable of reproduction. And we must know the length of time between births. The common porpoise is sexually adult at 15 months. The bottlenose dolphin reaches sexual maturity only at the age of 5 years. Among the large whales the age of puberty ranges between 4 and 6 years. When we compare these figures with those relating to much smaller land mammals (such as camels, zebras, and even seals), then we must admit that the large whales reach puberty at a youthful age.

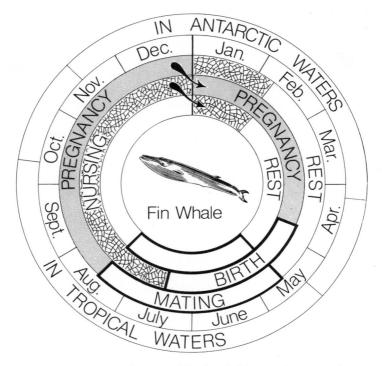

FIG. 76. Schematic diagram of the fin whale's reproductive cycle.

Female porpoises, dolphins, gray whales, and at least some humpback whales are fertile again immediately after giving birth or shortly thereafter. In the case of blue whales, fin whales, and sperm whales, most females do not ovulate during the period when they are nursing their young. On the average, then, these females give birth only once to a calf in each period of two years (Fig. 76). Laws has calculated that in order to achieve this result the fin whale ovulates an average of 2.8 times each period of two years, so that 2.8 *corpora albicantia* in the ovaries represent a period of two years of life. Unfortunately we are very poorly informed about the overall longevity of whales. But it is estimated that the life span of the large whales is 30 to 40 years; and we assume that whales, like other wild mammals, remain capable of procreation practically to the end of their lives although the interval between births may increase as they grow older. On this basis we can estimate that a given female bears a maximum of 10 to 12 calves during her lifetime. Thus the increment per animal comes to a maximum of 5 to 6. Naturally the real increment is much smaller because a certain number undoubtedly die in their first year, others die later of natural causes, and still others are killed by the whaling industry.

XII. *Whale Stock Preservation*

Each year the representatives of eighteen nations hold a meeting of the International Whaling Commission. The main topic of their discussions is almost always the same: How many whales should be allowed to be caught in Antarctic waters during the next hunting season? The aim of the commission and its advisory biologists is not to prevent the extermination of whales, as many people might think. The latter goal is rather the aim of international conservation organizations. In any case there is very little danger of any cetacean species being wholly exterminated by whaling in the Antarctic (see postscript). The exorbitant costs of a whaling expedition to the Antarctic Ocean mean that it simply would not be profitable unless a large number of whales could be caught.

The real aim of the International Whaling Commission is to prevent a diminution of the present-day stock, to ensure that this profitable source of oil, meat, and other valuable products will not be lost to our descendants. One related problem here is that the commission must also take an interest in the needs and interests of the various industries connected with whaling. Hence its motto is: "To save the whales without killing the industry." Moreover, since the interests of the participating nations often vary greatly, it is often quite difficult to reach a conclusion that is satisfactory to all.

133

In the 1930s the Antarctic whaling fleets hunted blue whales mainly. Now they hunt fin whales almost exclusively. This is due, in part, to the fact that the number of blue whales has obviously declined; in part, to the fact that certain conservation measures have been enacted; and in part, to the fact that whaling fleets no longer plunge as often and as deeply into the region of drift ice. Conservation measures have also been enacted with regard to the humpback whale. Thus present-day whalers and present-day (i.e., 1962) whale research concentrate mainly on the fin whale.

Obviously the decisions of the International Whaling Commission on the permissible catch each year must be based on precise knowledge of cetacean biology and, in particular, on what is called "population dynamics." The problem for biologists here is that they are not asked whether it is *desirable* to limit the catch but rather whether it is *absolutely necessary* to limit the catch. It is very easy to paint a catastrophic picture without good reason. Back in 1930, for example, Sir Sidney Harmer warned the Linnaean Society that the extinction of whales was only a few years away.

Until recently many whale researchers were of the opinion that the "Catchers Days Work" (C.D.W.) was an extremely reliable index of the state and trend of the whale stock. The C.D.W. measures the number of Blue Whale Units (1 blue whale = 2 fin whales = so and so many other species) caught by each whaler each day. From 1948 to 1959 this index has remained quite constant; only in the last two years was it noticeably lower. But quite recently a commission of fishery experts has pointed out that too few factors were taken into account in the C.D.W. index, and that the whole matter must be researched over again with more modern methods.

Estimates of the increase and decrease in the stock are easy to make when one has the following data at his disposal: the size of the present-day stock, the number of animals caught yearly, the natural mortality rate, and the number of animals born yearly. But of these factors only one is known precisely, i.e., the number of whales caught annually. We could get some idea of the size of the stock from an extensive marking effort. If 5 percent of the catch consisted of marked whales, then we could estimate that the total of marked animals in the catch represented about 5 percent of the stock. Unfortunately we are missing one factor in making this calculation. We do not know for what percentage of the marked animals the markers are not recovered for one reason or another. Moreover, an estimate of the size of the stock, based on the sightings of the English research ship "Discovery II," can only provide a very superficial idea. In addition these sightings stem from the 1930s. It is quite possible that the stock of fin whales has increased since then, because the stock of blue whales declined and more food has been available to the fin whales.

Needless to say, it is almost impossible to collect direct data on the natural mortality of the whales. We have the impression that in the case of cetaceans, as in the case of other large mammals, the mortality rate is greatest in the first year of life. In that year, a certain percentage of the animals perish from the weaning process, parasites, or predators (killer whales); among land mammals the figure is 15 to 50 percent. Now and then older whales may run into catastrophic situations, as figure 77 shows; but natural mortality is extremely low in these years. Fatal diseases seem to be rare. When 12,000 whales were examined by British meat inspectors, only two were labelled unsafe because of disease. There is also the fact that whales and dolphins with severe wounds or skeletal diseases, which must cause them great difficulty in eating and moving about, can live for many years. This indicates that their overall biological condition is extremely good.

FIG. 77. In the Crown Prince Gustave Channel (near Graham Land) an English expedition to the South Pole found a number of lesser rorquals which could not get to the open sea. With great effort the whales were still able to keep a few holes open, but their fate was sealed. Note the vapor cloud and the drawn-in floor of the mouth during exhalation.

In other words, they have few enemies and a rich supply of food (Fig. 78).

One can get indirect information on cetacean mortality (natural or man-caused) by preparing an age-distribution chart of the whales that have been caught. If one knows the percentage of one-year-olds, two-year-olds, three-year-olds, etc. in the stock, and if one can draw up a chart for several successive years, then one can draw certain conclusions about the stock's increase or decrease by noting the increase or decrease of youngsters and oldsters. There is one difficulty with this method: the catch must be a

FIG. 78. A makeshift joint has formed in the healing of a fractured lower jaw of a sperm whale. Photo by N. J. Teljer.

representative sample of the stock. In other words, the catch must be a completely random sample and whalers must not make any deliberate choices of their own. But there is sharp competition in the whaling industry today, so it is quite likely that the whalers do make deliberate choices because younger, more inexperienced whales can be caught more easily than older ones.

Moreover, the reliability of this method depends completely on the reliability of the age determination. Up to now three methods have been used to determine cetacean age. Professor Ruud of Oslo has pointed out that there is a certain periodicity in the pattern of density to be found in the baleens as they run from their basis in the gum to their tip (where they are used most). This pattern of periodicity can be judged in terms of annual rings (Fig. 79). Van Utrecht developed a modification of this method in Amsterdam. She uses a divergent division of the years and takes into account the portion of the baleen

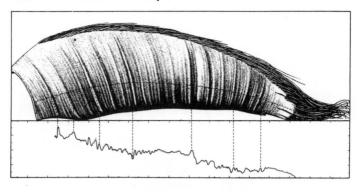

FIG. 79. Baleens of a blue whale with a periodicity graph based on Ruud's method. A different division is used in Amsterdam.

located in the gum. In general the second method leads to a higher age count.

It has been shown that the methods are reliable only up to an age of about 3 to 4 years because above this age a greatly varying number of periods disappear completely through wear and tear. But the modified method did concur very satisfactorily with the conclusions of Laws (England), who determined that there was an increase of 2.8 *corpora albicantia* every two years in the ovaries of a female who had reached puberty (see chapter 11). Thus when one has determined the age of puberty through one of the first two methods mentioned above, one can then determine the age of the adult female animal by means of the ovaries.

The third method was described by Purves (London) for the first time in 1955. It is based on "ear plugs" that are found in the inside of the external auditory canal of rorquals (Fig. 80). They are peglike structures about 20 centimeters long. On their longitudinal sections they have a number of layers running parallel to each other with alternating light and dark color. These layers are taken

FIG. 80. Two "ear plugs" of a fin whale. On the longitudinal section (right) one can see the annual rings. Photo by W. L. van Utrecht (Amsterdam).

to be annual rings. Initially experts were of the opinion that two of these bands formed in a single year. But in the 1959 season a Japanese whaler gathered "ear plugs" from animals which had been marked in the 1930s and whose minimum age was therefore known. As a result we may have to work on the basis of 1 to 2 layers per year. Moreover, it is very difficult to determine the age of animals from one to five years old with this method.

Another unfortunate fact is that as yet we have not been able to test the reliability of the first two methods on a fin whale whose exact age was known. So up to now doubts remain about the reliability of all the methods mentioned.

What we have said above indicates that our knowledge of cetacean biology has not advanced far enough to enable us to provide the whaling industry with a sound and solid expert opinion on how many whales may be caught each year. But our knowledge has increased substantially in recent decades so that cetacean biology may reasonably hope to provide the desired answer to this important question in the near future.

Postscript

JOHN E. BARDACH, *Director*
Hawaii Institute of Marine Biology
University of Hawaii

Going, Going, Gone

Professor Slijper published his classical but still defini-
tive book on the biology of whales and dolphins in 1962.
He ended the treatise with a short section on concerns
about the stocks of whales. He briefly mentions the International Whaling Commission of, then, 18 whaling nations, with its self-imposed charge, "To save the whales
without killing the industry." Only a decade later it had
become clear that the commission had failed; that the industry had virtually killed itself, and that it had been
instrumental in the probable extinction of the blue whale,
the largest animal that ever lived. Furthermore the industry had hunted down the other species of baleen
whales to a state of severe and rapid depletion. Only the
toothed sperm whale may still be saved as a substantial
resource if the two remaining major whaling nations,
Japan and the USSR, adhere to the strictest conservation
measures. In the light of these two countries' actions in
the Whaling Commission and in view of the apparent
inability or unwillingness of nations to embark on long-
term enlightened conservation measures, even the last
of the large whales, which still yields tens of thousands

of carcasses per year, stands in jeopardy of being severely overfished, and eventually also of being depleted like his, predominantly Antarctic, baleen whale cousins.

It would be simple to say that the reason for the sad fate of the whales, especially in the last ten years, is greed and man's general tendency to take the cash and let the credit go. But leaving it at that would preclude discussion of an interesting chapter of modern man's interaction with the natural world and one from which we may yet learn some useful lessons.

To do so we must consider several aspects of the situation such as the whaling statistics of the last two decades, the over-capitalization of the whale fishery which led to the rapid acquisition of the technical power for whale overkill, the actions of the Whaling Commission, especially those of its most influential members, and finally the basic assumptions under which common or truly international management of a widely roaming renewable marine resource would be possible.

Whaling Statistics and the Case of the Blue Whale

The season of 1961–62 marked the peak of post World War II Antarctic whaling, as indicated in table 1. Even then blue whales were becoming scarce; their portion in the catch dropped to less than half of what it had been in 1953. Small (1971) states that in 1963 there may have been only about 600 regular blue whales left in the Antarctic, and that 84 percent of the females among them were probably sexually immature. Some of them matured and reproduced. Consequently, it was still possible that 700 animals fell to the gunners' harpoons in subsequent years before complete protection of blue whales from pelagic whalers throughout the Antarctic became a reality in 1965.

We do not know how many dozens or hundreds of blue whales are still alive today. Some say that it cannot be

TABLE 1

Number of Whales Caught: World

	1953–54	1961–62	1962–63	1963–64	1964–65	1965–66	1966–67	1967–68	1968–69
Blue	3,009	1,255	1,429	372	613	243	70	—	—
Finback	31,335	30,178	21,916	19,182	12,317	6,882	6,458	5,268	5,659
Humpback	3,155	2,436	2,758	318	452	59	4	2	—
Other baleen whales	2,573	8,905	9,618	13,874	25,750	23,329	19,282	17,295	11,637
Sperm	13,543	23,316	27,858	29,255	25,548	27,378	26,424	24,080	21,471
Total	53,615	66,090	63,579	63,001	64,680	57,891	52,238	46,645	37,768

Adapted from *FAO Yearbook of Fishery Statistics*, Vol. 28, 1969.

more than 200 but even if there are a hundred or so more, chances for the recovery of the species are slim indeed, even assuming complete protection and absence of hunting.

Let us take the figure of 200 and assume that half of them are males and the other half females. Let us further assume from the data on sexual maturity of females in 1963 and from the researches of Professor Slijper and others that 10 percent of each sex have become mature in each subsequent year and have found each other. Ten pairs of blue whales would then breed every year and, disregarding infant mortality, they would produce five blue whale calves. As these mature they must, in turn, find a mate. There are about nine million square miles of feeding territory between the Antarctic convergence and the ice cap. If the calves were evenly distributed each one of them would occupy an area of 1.8 million square miles. Even with their phenomenal range of sound communication the calves would face a well nigh impossible task in satisfying their urge to mate. If the young are not evenly distributed and if by chance several females or several males only frequented a small area, probabilities of mating success would vary a little, but they would still be extremely low.

We have assumed no infant mortality, which is obviously wrong, but we do not know what the rate is. Nor can we assume that no blue whales were shot after 1965. Some nations with whaling bases on land—Chile, Ecuador, and Peru—left the International Whaling Commission in 1952. It is perfectly "legal" for them to still hunt blue whales. In fact there is a joint Japanese-Chilean whaling venture, using Japanese ships and personnel. This neat arrangement permitted the Japanese in 1967, to concur in the Whaling Commission's ban on blue whale killing anywhere south of the equator, and still ship whale products to Japan, being in a strict legal sense, exempt from any possible international censure or counter measure, except possibly that of their own conscience.

Only the next few decades, in fact only the next century will tell if the blue whale is now extinct, if it will vanish a few years from now, or if by any chance it can miraculously increase its population again. Other, albeit far less depleted species, the right and sperm whales—quarries of the less efficient whaling fleets of the last century—have a more restricted range than the blue whale, and breeding associations that are more favorable for survival. They did make a come-back, the former less successfully so than the latter.

Whaling statistics for the other baleen whale species show the same trend that could be observed for the blues even in the 1950s (see table 1). Finbacks are in steady decline and the humpback is virtually no more. Catches of the smaller sei whales passed their peak in 1966 and 1967. Obviously the reproductive potential of the species could not keep pace with the hunting pressure.

Yet the man-caused depletion of baleen whales has opened an interesting possibility of marine resource utilization that is connected with the whales. Their main food was—and for those which remain still is—krill. Although krill converters are efficient, their conversion efficiencies are still subject to laws of ecology and physiology. That is to say that what remains of materials and energy ingested by an animal is only a fraction—usually not more than 20 percent—of the amount fed upon. The rest is dissipated in the day-to-day upkeep of the feeder. Thus, if we were able to harvest krill and turn it into useful, that is palatable and acceptable food, we would get more for our money than by harvesting whales.

The problem is, in part, a biological-oceanographic and, in part, a technological one. Its biological aspects lie in our ability to locate, better than the whales, enough krill concentrations to warrant investment in large scale harvesting. The technical aspects, aside from inventing economical krill catching devices, lie in turning the crustaceans which have a high oil and high carotenoid pigment content into products people will eat. Some good beginnings have been made by Japanese and Soviet researchers. The Soviet Union, for instance, now markets frozen krill cakes called Okean, and it seems that the Russian people accept the product, at least on a trial basis. If we make substantial headway in this endeavor in the next few years, we might even compete with the whales for their food and we may, although this is uncertain, evolve toward a state of affairs where whaling for baleen whales will not be the worthwhile pursuit it once was. At the same time we would have to ascertain whether we would reduce the recovery potential of baleen whales by doing them out of part or perhaps much of their food. In the long run the problem may even shift from baleen whale to krill conservation. Present world population trends and ongoing technological developments make this a distinct possibility.

Today sperm whales furnish the bulk of whale catches (see table 1). As one would expect, they represent real conservation problems. The Russian cetologist Berzin states that in the 1966–67 season in the Antarctic and in the calendar year 1967 in other regions of the world ocean, 12 countries (16 flotillas, 26 shore stations, and 250 whaling vessels) captured 25,921 sperm whales, more than 50 percent (14,775 specimens) being taken by Soviet whalers. For the other countries, see table 2 for the distribution of the catches.

But even this bounty is on the decline; the catches from 1966 to 1969 show a slow but steady drop and also a gradual decrease of the size of the animals. In the 1937–38 season the average sperm whale in the Antarctic measured 16.2 m; in 1965–66 they were only 13.8 meters long,

TABLE 2

Country	Number of Sperms	Country	Number of Sperms
Japan	6,007	Portugal	395
So. African		Canada	306
Republic	2,256	Spain	207
Norway	617	United	
Australia	586	States	100[*]
Chile	533	Brazil	20

[*] The United States have now ceased all whaling and imposed a ban on the trading of whale products.

SOURCE: Berzin, *The Sperm Whale*, 1972.

indicating that progressively younger and younger animals were being hunted.

Sperm whales are very social animals. The males have harems with the smaller of them, which engage in the breeding—probably because sperm whale females are substantially smaller than the largest known males. The larger males leave the herds and migrate toward the Arctic and Antarctic. Thus Berzin (1971) suggests that: "Rational economically viable whaling of male sperm whales in the northern and southern waters (above 50°) can be carried out on a large scale. In case of excessive catches in these waters the average length (and age) of the animals will reach that at which the male sperms leave the harems (about 12 m) and it will fluctuate around this size, whereas a deterioration in the state of the reserves can be expressed only in the decrease in the number of adults taken." But he adds, "that this will be only on condition that whaling be stopped in both hemispheres at latitudes below 40°."

Few nations would have to agree to such regulations with eight of the eleven listed by Berzin being members of the International Whaling Commission. Perhaps the commission will do with this last remaining exploitable species what it did not achieve with the others, namely, to preserve it in such a way that an industry, but surely on a smaller than the present scale, could still operate.

The Whaling Industry and the Whaling Commission

As Slijper points out and Bardach (1970) amplifies, accounts of whaling in the northern seas go back to the time of King Alfred in the ninth century. By the thirteenth century, it was an important industry among the Basques. By 1550 the English and the Dutch had set up shore stations on Spitsbergen for rendering whale blubber. They pursued whales with 200-ton sailing vessels that carried several pinnaces (light vessels rowed by 48 oarsmen). Whaling stations were the forerunners of later Antarctic shore factories and had such amenities as spirit depots, bakeries, inns, and churches. American whaling developed during the seventeenth and eighteenth centuries and had reached its heyday by 1850 when a fleet of over 700 sailing vessels pursued certain whales over all the world's oceans.

The species hunted by the Basques and the Dutch, known as the Basque right whale and the Greenland right whale, respectively, are shorter and sturdier creatures than the blue whale and, unlike most other species, remain afloat after being killed, hence the word "right." Right whales are also supposedly slower and more peaceable than the others. The carcasses either were towed to shore stations or, as whalers ventured farther out to sea, were lashed to the side of the ship, so that the blubber could be peeled and rendered into oil in a brick furnace aboard the ship. At times the furnace was stocked with the refuse of the whale itself; the stench and gore aboard a whaling ship out of Nantucket or New Bedford must have been very distinctive.

In place of right whales, early in the eighteenth century, the Massachusetts whalers began to hunt sperm
whales. They not only floated after being killed but
yielded, in addition to the oil from the blubber, the
highly prized oil from the cavity in the head, along with
spermaceti, which was used for making candles and
pomades, and an occasional clump of ambergris. However, only baleen whales yielded whalebone, which was
used in making stays for ladies' undergarments. The most
important product of all, though, was the oil, which was
burned in lamps until petroleum began to take its place.
The right and sperm whales were hunted relentlessly, and
their numbers became fewer and fewer. As a consequence,
traditional methods of whaling declined because it had
become a poor risk for capital investment.

The whalers of the nineteenth century had seen blue
whales and their somewhat smaller cousins, the fin whale
and the rorqual, of which the latter sometimes occurred
in north temperate seas. These whales were too fast to be
pursued by sail and oar. The hunt for them came with
the harnessing of steam, then diesel power, and finally
the invention of the explosive harpoon, patented in 1870
by the Norwegian Svend Foyn. Since then the harpoon
has been modified only slightly and has been used to
kill many hundreds of thousands of whales.

In the Southern Hemisphere, whaling stations were
first operated around the turn of the century and pelagic
whaling from factory ships was first tried in 1923. It sky-
rocketed during the years between the two wars and has
been going strong ever since, though by now, it may be
near collapse. A factory ship such as the *Sovjetskaya
Russia,* built for the USSR, displaces up to 44,000 tons
and is equipped with a movie theater, hospital, and library, as well as with devilishly efficient machinery for
disposing of the carcass of any whale that is pulled
aboard. Within half an hour a 50-foot leviathan can be

made to vanish from the deck and into the open maws of pressure cookers, meat grinders, freezers, and so on. Attached to the mother ship are a flotilla of catchers between 100 and 150 feet long, high-bowed, fast, and seaworthy. The harpoon is mounted on the bow platform and is reached from the bridge by a gangway that is almost always slippery and often covered with ice. From the platform the master gunner aims the barbed shaft with its explosive head at the whale's body from a distance of about 50 yards. Great skill is needed to guide the vessel within shooting distance and to gauge the whale's undulating path as it rises to the surface to breathe. Blue whales, finbacks, and rorquals—species that sink soon after death—are heaved to with the catcher's powerful winch, inflated with compressed air, studded with a radio buoy, and cast adrift to be picked up later.

Early whaling clearly pitted human courage and relatively nonmechanized skills against a formidable foe. Added to Svend Foyn's invention of the harpoon, factory ships, helicopter pilots that guide catcher boats by radio, radar, and other electronic guiding devices tipped the scales. The whales did not have a chance unless man were to protect the whales from himself. But man had evolved the tenet that the whales, being creatures of the open sea, belonged to no one and therefore to all. Highly effective whaling could only be carried out by technologically advanced nations to whom the whales could supply all the goods depicted on page 11, especially meat and oil. Yet several of these nations dropped out of the race one by one; even the Norwegians who had dominated whaling for so long saw the self-defeating nature of the contest. Japan, with its traditional reliance on the resources of the sea and with dire postwar needs for food and oil, and the USSR, which had elected to mold itself into one of the world's most powerful fishing nations, continued to build, and in fact, overbuild their whaling capabilities.

Factory ships increased and with them their flotillas of catcher boats; but their efficiency declined.

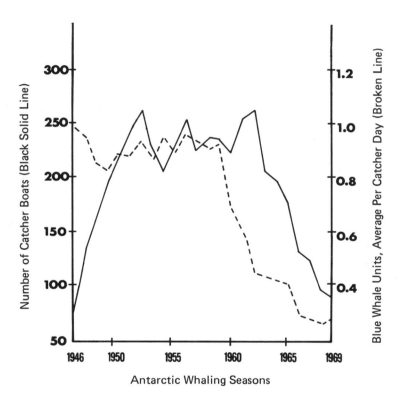

FIG. 81. Catcher-Boat Efficiency, 1946–1969. (Adapted from Michael D. Bradley, "The International Whaling Commission: Allocating an International Pelagic Ocean Resource," 1971.)

One should note here particularly that there was a sharp drop in blue whale units per catcher day before the largest number of catcher boats were in the field. But investment in so much hardware with the commitment to the employment of thousands of people in all phases of the industry had their own momentum (or so the executives of large whaling companies or leaders of state enterprises must have felt). This economic driving force seems to have influenced the policies of Japan and the USSR in the Whaling Commission where, as we will see, it was not difficult to hold out for larger than sensible yearly quotas.

No figures from investment and return are available from Soviet whaling enterprises but Japanese data suggest (Bradley, 1971) that the two dominant fishing companies which derived only 8.5 and 16 percent of their total sales from whaling, respectively, had annual whaling revenues of about 525 million dollars in the mid-sixties between them (calculated at the 1965 yen-dollar exchange rate). Such moneys represent commensurate investments and businessmen or commissars have to look toward the amortization of that investment. They will continue to exploit a dwindling resource with the hope that it will hold up for a few years longer and/or that new resources will become available. This has happened inasmuch as whale flotillas, having worked primarily in the Antarctic, fanned out into other whaling grounds of the Atlantic and the Pacific only now to find that stocks began to dwindle there as well.

Of course, anyone could plainly see, even before World War II, that the whales would lose out and therefore the businessmen would too. The results of this recognition, long in coming as it was, led to the establishment of an International Whaling Convention in 1946, and stemming from it, a body that would regulate whaling, the International Whaling Commission. (Earlier limited whaling regulations had been properly signed into a convention by the League of Nations in 1932; they were observed by Norway and Great Britain but disregarded by all other member nations.)

The preamble to the 1946 convention established and defined the objectives of the commission in general terms. The intentions were good; conservation measures were to be held in tune with development exigencies. Limited exploitation, recovery periods, and the like were considered. The convention contained a schedule dealing with minimum lengths, seasons, and specialized areas. These could be changed by the commission according to need. There were also provisions not subject to change by the commission such as details of operational structure, duties of governments to enforce regulations, and the like.

Each signatory nation had one commissioner and one or more experts in the commission which is, in essence, an autonomous body, and thus formal diplomatic convocation is not necessary to conduct its business.

Small (1971) describes its operations as follows:

The passage of a proposed amendment by the Whaling Commission required an affirmative vote of three-fourths of the commissioners voting. For a period of 90 days thereafter every member nation had the right to submit an objection to the Commission and not be subject to the amendment. When that occurred every other member nation had an additional 90-day period during which it too might lodge an objection and not be bound by the amendment. This procedure amounted to an absolute right of veto over any proposal made in the Commission. In practice this caused an objection by one nation to be followed by objections from all other whaling nations even if they had originally voted for the amendment in question and even if it meant abandoning a conservation measure they were willing to accept. For example, Nation A proposes a ban on the killing of blue whales in Antarctic Area II and the measure passes by a three-fourths vote. Nation B lodges an objection and is not bound by the amendment. Nation A must in turn lodge a similar objection or its whalers will be forbidden to kill blue whales there while the whalers of Nation B are free to do so. (You can almost predict the fate of most attempts to reduce the Antarctic catch when it is recalled that the Japanese Commissioner to the Whaling Commission was a representative of the Japanese whaling companies.) In actual practice objections were not very numerous. Before a proposed amendment was ready for a vote the commissioners usually knew the opinions of their colleagues. If one nation was adamantly opposed to it, a subsequent objection would render it null and void. Under those conditions the proposal was either retracted or watered down to suit the objecting nation.

The right to lodge an objection, to veto any conservation proposal, was the greatest weakness of the International Whaling Commission. This was foreseen at the Washington Conference when the International Whaling Commission was being proposed, and it was debated at great length. Norway and the United Kingdom opposed the right of objection and wanted all amendments passed by the Commission to be binding on all members. The American delegate, who made the original proposal, defended the veto as a valuable "safety valve." Because of the veto a nation that felt seriously inconvenienced by a proposed amendment did not have to leave the Commission and thereby become free of all controls. Such a nation could veto the objectionable proposal, remain a member of the Commission, and be subject to all the other regulations then in force. The alternative to the right to object, argued the American delegate, would lead to no international controls at all. The conference voted unanimously to retain the veto right of all member nations.

The right to object to any new proposal did achieve the result predicted by the American delegate even though it did preclude success for the International Whaling Commission. Every pelagic whaling nation joined the Commission precisely because it could prevent any serious restraints being placed on its whalers. There were, however, a few nations with a land-based whaling industry that refused to sign the Convention and become members of the International Whaling Commission. The most important of such nations were Chile, Ecuador, and Peru that formed their own regulatory organization known as the Commission for the South Pacific. Those nations refused to join the international effort because they considered the regulations in the original schedule too restrictive. For many years the International Whaling Commission attempted in vain to induce Chile, Ecuador, and Peru to join it and abandon their own organization. In 1966 they replied that in view of the abysmal failure of the Whaling Commission to preserve the Antarctic whale stocks it would be more appropriate for it to join their Commission for the South Pacific.

Another weakness of the International Whaling Commission was its lack of authority to limit the number of factory ships or to allocate a quota to any of them. Article V of the International Convention for the Regulation of Whaling specifically denied the Commission that authority. Any nation was free to increase the number of its pelagic fleets if warranted by favorable domestic conditions, economic or political. As we have seen, Japan and the Soviet Union did precisely that.

Some nations could not decrease the number of their fleets to a commensurate degree because of financial and technical limitations inherent to the industry. The result was an increasing number of whaling fleets hunting fewer and fewer whales. This situation was foreseen at the 1946 Washington Conference, but no serious efforts were made to avert it. To have given the Whaling Commission authority to limit the number of factory ships would have violated the principle of the freedom of the seas that grants to every nation the right to use the resources of the high seas as it decides. Furthermore, the right of veto would have rendered useless any authority to limit the number of factory ships. Had the authority been granted to the commission and the right of veto denied to the members, few if any nations would have remained members for very long. Any nation so limited would have withdrawn from the convention and the others would inevitably have done the same. During the short discussion of this crucial matter at the Washington Conference, the American delegate presented a unique argument against the granting of such powers of control to the International Whaling Commission: "The United States Government has taken the position that such allocation is not in the interest of free and competitive enterprise and it is not necessary to the conservation of whaling resources."

With the veto rule as outlined and the commission's reluctance to restrict the number of whaling ships across the board and with at least one, if not more, of the commission members being very clearly spokesman for the industry (if not, in fact, in the industry's employ when not attending a commission meeting) it was not surprising that unfillable quotas were set again and again even until the early seventies. It has been said that the stocks of whales would have been depleted earlier had there been no convention and no commission, but that is small consolation. The commission's greatest shortcoming was that too many of its members equated national economic interests with that for the preservation of the resource. They did not consider that such preservation of a living resource should be for the common good, and that it is only possible if the perpetuation of the animals under exploitation, and not the industry, is considered paramount.

On the Regulation of Living Marine Resources

Over millenia mankind developed certain concepts of ownership of land, water, fish, and game. The latter two, if not on private preserves or in ponds guarded by slaves, were called *res nullius* by the Romans, a law-minded people who have bequeathed to us a good many bases for our own legal notions. As long as there were not too many people going after these bounties of nature, the consequences were workable of declaring fish as belonging to no one—at least not until they had been captured by someone who then became the owner. True this led to man-of-war-supported rivalries in the past, such as those over herring between the Hanseatic League and the Dutch, and the Dutch and the British. By and large things did not work out too badly, mainly because the richness of the seas as provider of free protein fare (you don't need to grow it, you only harvest it) seemed unlimited, at least until the latter part of the nineteenth century when man's numbers increased meteorically and when ships and gear became ever more efficient. Then scientists began to warn us about too heavy fishing pressures on various stocks, and advocated a more international approach to the overfishing problem. Many fish stocks have dwindled since then, some due to natural events such as hydrographic changes, more to heavy fishing, and some to a combination of both. Few nations of like mind and needs, such as the United States and Canada, have managed to reach agreement on joint sustained-yield control of the American West Coast halibut fishery. Other fisheries undertaken by several nations like those of the western North Atlantic have a more "free for all" characteristic, some limited agreements notwithstanding.

Perhaps because successful sea fishing now relies on an advanced technology, there is a tendency among developing nations to wish to extend their territorial limits far out to sea, as far as 200 miles. This seems to be the trend in the preparations for a forthcoming international law of the sea conference. International waters would shrink and the roaming of fish or whales would coincide with the boundaries of nations even less than they do today. Understandable as the reasons for such boundary extensions may be, they seem a bit anachronistic in a shrinking world and in no way conducive to the best and most peaceful management of what could be an ongoing source of food and riches for mankind.

The oceans can be looked at as the common heritage of man, all rivers drain into it and carry nutrients from the land into the sea. These nutrients go through marine foodchains, and most of them later find their way into the intermediate and deep layers of the oceans. There they remain for millenia but eventually they are returned to the surface for the sun's rays to make them give rise to life again. These cycles are long, and first terrestrial or national origins of nutrient molecules cannot be detected. This is only one of the reasons—their far and wide roaming is another—why many sea animals, certainly those of off-shore upwelling and mid-oceanic regions, should be considered humanity's common property, to be apportioned by need rather than power and greed.

Can such utopian goals be achieved? Certainly in theory, inasmuch as a world fish authority with one or several agent nations that undertake the fishing for it has been advocated. Historic rights and needs might still be recognized in such a management scheme, but most importantly, an international authority, as Christy and Scott (1965) point out, could operate more cheaply than individual nations. They could buy both labor capital inputs at low prices or interest rates while they could still sell part of the catch at highest prices. Presumably working within an economy of large scale, the authority could search for and test new techniques, and being international, it could phase out, early and with relatively little hardship, agreements which may have served too few. The authority's zone of jurisdiction is not likely to include the truly coastal zones of nations, but it would still comprise large parts of the oceans. In it no one would be able to say, "If we don't get these fish someone else will"; they would be apportioned according to true protein needs.

In practice, though, things threaten to be different; and enough preliminary meetings to the earlier mentioned law of the sea conference have been held to sense the pressure among the developing nations, for extension of fishery territorial limits far out to sea.

The likely portends of this scenario are not enlightened long-range management of all harvestable products of the sea in the common interest of mankind. The nation states which would control broad strips of sea along their shores would fortify themselves against intruders, but since neither fish nor whales learn to respect boundaries set by man, inter- or multi-national agreements will still be necessary. Unless these are resource—instead of nation-oriented—they will be to little avail, as were the whaling regulations of the past. On the remaining high seas there will be fiercer competition than there is today for shrinking resources for an expanding population. Unless some social invention such as an international fishing authority, or an even broader ocean use and resources authority, comes into being, it is almost certain that the exploiters of the high seas will remain the technologically advanced nations of the world—those who have not only fewer mouths to feed than the rest of mankind, but who are also less needy of animal protein fare. It appears to be almost a foregone conclusion that their nets and ships will compete with the whales for food as well as relentlessly hunt all the fish and the whales—if there are any left to be hunted.

Classification of the Cetaceans

Only the most important subdivisions and species are indicated here.

I. Ancient whale ancestors, *Archaeoceti.*
Upper Eocene–Upper Oligocene. Differentiated denture. Nasal opening usually not on top of the head. Skull symmetrical. 2–20 meters.

II. Baleen or whalebone whales, *Mystacoceti.*
Middle Oligocene–Recent. Baleens. Nasal opening on top of the head. Skull symmetrical.

    A. Right whales, *Balaenidae.*
Upper Miocene–Recent. Long baleens, no dorsal fin, no grooves.

        1. Greenland right whale, *Balaena mysticetus* L. 16 meters. Arctic Ocean. Alternate name: bowhead whale.

        2. Biscayan right whale, *Eubalaena glacialis* Bonnat (*E. australis* Desm.). 15 meters. Worldwide except in the tropics.

        3. Pigmy right whale, *Caperea* (or *Neobalaena*) *marginata* (Gray). 6 meters. Antarctica.

    B. Gray whales, *Eschrichtiidae* (*Rhachianectidae*).
Postglacial–Recent. Short baleens, no dorsal fin, 2–4 grooves.

        1. California gray whale, *Eschrichtius* (*Rhachianectes*) *glaucus* Cope. 13 meters. North Pacific. Alternate names: devil fish; mussel digger.

    C. Rorquals, *Balaenopteridae.*
Upper Miocene–Recent. Short baleens, 70–100 grooves, dorsal fin.

        1. Blue whale, *Balaenoptera musculus* (L.), 24 meters. Worldwide. Alternate names: sulphur-bottom whale; finback whale.

2. Fin whale, *Balaenoptera physalus* (L.), 21 meters. Worldwide. Alternate names: finner; common rorqual.

3. Sei whale, *Balaenoptera borealis* (Lesson), 15 meters. Worldwide. Alternate names: coal fish; pollack.

4. Bryde's whale, *Balaenoptera brydei* (Olsen), 13 meters. Tropics and subtropics.

5. Lesser rorqual, *Balaenoptera acutorostrata* Lacép., 9 meters. Worldwide, but rarer in the tropics. Alternate names: little piked whale; Minke whale; sharp-headed finner.

6. Humpback whale, *Megaptera novaeangliae* Borowski (*M. nodosa* Bonnat), 14 meters. Worldwide. Alternate names: hump whale; bunch whale.

III. Toothed whales, *Odontoceti.*

Upper Eocene—Recent. In the more recent groups, denture is composed of uniform teeth. Nasal opening on top of the skull, usually on top of the head as well. Skull of the more recent groups is asymmetrical.

A. Sperm whales, *Physeteridae.*

Upper Miocene—Recent. Reduced denture. Cuttlefish-eaters.

1. Sperm whale, *Physeter macrocephalus* L., 18 meters. Worldwide. Alternate names: cachelot; pothead whale; spermaceti whale.

2. Pigmy Sperm whale, *Kogia breviceps* (Blainv.), 4 meters. Worldwide.

B. Beaked whales, *Ziphiidae.*

Upper Miocene—Recent. Denture reduced to 1 or 2 visible teeth. Cuttlefish-eaters.

1. Bottlenose whale, *Hyperoodon ampullatus* (Forster), 9 meters. North Atlantic. In the Antarctic: *Hyperoodon planifrons* Forster.

2. Beaked whales, *Mesoplodon.* Nine species. Worldwide genus.

C. River dolphins, *Platanistidae.*

Upper Miocene—Recent. Long, slender snout. Fish-eaters. River dwellers. 4 species in the Ganges and Indus, Mekong, the Amazon, the Rio de la Plata, and Tung Ting Lake (China) respectively. 1.50 to 2.50 meters.

D. Ocean dolphins, *Delphinapteridae.*
   Pleistocene—Recent. No visible dorsal fin. Fish-eaters.
   1. Beluga whale, *Delphinapterus leucas* (Pallas),
      4.50 meters. Arctic Ocean. Alternate name: white
      whale.
   2. Narwhal, *Monodon Monoceros* L., 5 meters. Arctic Ocean.
E. Porpoises, *Phocaenidae.*
   Miocene—Recent. Dorsal fin. Spadelike teeth. No
   snout. Fish-eaters.
   1. Common porpoise, *Phocaena phocaena* (L.), 1.50
      meters. North Atlantic. Alternate name: harbor
      porpoise.
   2. Indian porpoise, *Neomeris phocaenoides* (Cuv.),
      1.30 meters. Indian and Pacific Oceans.
F. Dolphins, *Delphinidae.*
   Miocene—Recent. Usually have clearcut dorsal fin
   and snout. Conical teeth. Mainly fish-eaters.
   1. Killer whale, *Orcinus orca* (L.), 9 meters. Worldwide.
   2. False killer whale, *Pseudorca crassidens* (Owen),
      5 meters. Worldwide.
   3. Pilot whale, *Globicephala melaena* (Traill), 8 meters.
      North Atlantic. Represented by other species
      in other seas. Alternate name: blackfish.
   4. Risso's whale, *Grampus griseus* Cuv., 3 meters.
      Worldwide.
   5. Bottlenose dolphin, *Tursiops truncatus* (Mont.),
      3.50 meters. Probably worldwide. Several races.
   6. Common dolphin, *Delphinus delphis* L., 2.25 meters.
      Worldwide in warm and temperate waters.
      Alternate name: saddle-backed dolphin.
   7. White-sided dolphin, *Lagenorhynchus.* Genus
      worldwide with several species and races. 1.50–3
      meters.
   8. Spotted dolphin, *Stenella.* Several species between
      50°N and 40°S. 1.0–2.5 meters. Alternate name:
      long-snouted dolphin.

For further reading:

Dr. Slijper provides an in-depth treatment of this same subject in a more extensive work which has been translated into

English. See E. J. Slijper, *Whales: The Biology of Cetaceans.* Trans. A. J. Pomerans, New York: Basic Books, 1962.

REFERENCES

Bardach, John E. *Harvest of the Sea.* New York and Evanston: Harper & Row Publ., 1970.

Berzin, A. A. *The Sperm Whale.* Edited by A. V. Yablakov, Israel Program for Scientific Translations. U.S. Department of Commerce, Springfield, Va.: Technical Information Service, 1972.

Bradley, Michael D. "The International Whaling Commission: Allocating an International Pelagic Ocean Resource." Ph.D. dissertation, University of Michigan, 1971.

Christy, Francis T. Jr., and Anthony, Scott. *The Common Wealth in Ocean Fisheries.* Baltimore, Md.: The Johns Hopkins Press, 1965.

FAO Yearbook of Fishery Statistics, Vol. 28. Rome, Italy: Food & Agriculture Organization of IL United Nations, 1969.

Small, George L. *The Blue Whale.* London and New York: Columbia University Press, 1971.

Picture Credits

Illustrations not from the author's own files are from the following sources:

Figs. 1, 8, 9, 10, 11, 12, 14, 19, 21, 22, 25, 27, 28, 30, 38, 43, 45, 53, 54, 55, 60, 68, 71, 72, 74, 75, 78, 79. Slijper, E. J., *Walvissen*, Amsterdam: D. B. Centen, 1958. See note on further reading at end of cetacean classification chart in this volume.

Fig. 7. Müller, H. C., *Archiv für Naturgeschichte*, 1920 A.

Figs. 13, 44, 57, 58. Beneden, P. J. van, and P. Gervais, *Osteographie des Cétacés*, Paris, 1880.

Fig. 18. Glassell, A. C., *Natural History*, 1953, 62:63.

Fig. 24. Andrews, R. C., *Memoirs Americ. Mus. Nat. Hist.*, N. S., 1914, 1:239.

Fig. 26. Heezen, B. C., *Norsk Hvalfangst Tidende*, 1957, 46:665.

Fig. 33. Breschet, G., *Histoire anatomique d'un organe de nature vasculaire dans les Cétacés*, Paris: Bechet Jeune, 1836.

Fig. 37. Dillin, J. W., *Natural History*, 1952, 61:152.

Fig. 39. Hill, R. N., *Window in the Sea*, London: Gollancz Ltd., 1957.

Fig. 41. Siebenaler, J. B., and D. K. Caldwell, *Journ. Mammalogy*, 1956, 37:126.

Fig. 46. Norris, K. S., c.s., *Biological Bulletin*, 1961, 120:163.

Fig. 47. Slijper, E. J., *Mens en Huisdier*, 2nd ed., Zutphen: Thieme, 1948.

Fig. 49. Mackintosh, N. A., and J. F. G. Wheeler, *Discovery Reports*, 1942, 1:197.

Fig. 59. Pernkopf, E., c.s. In Bolk's *Handbuch der vergleichenden Anatomie der Wirbeltiere*, 1937, III, 349.

Fig. 61. Anthony, R., *Mem. Inst. Espanol. Ocean.*, 1922, 3/2a:35.

Fig. 62. Marr, J. W. S., *Norsk Hvalfangst Tidende,* 1956, 45:127.

Fig. 65. Brown, S. G., *Discovery Reports,* 1954, 26:355.

Fig. 66. Nishiwaki, M., and K. Hayashi, *Scient. Rep. Whales. Res. Inst. Tokyo,* 1950, 3:183.

Fig. 70. Wislocki, G. B., *Biological Bulletin,* 1933, 65:81.

Index

167